JEREMIAH PROPHET UNDER SIEGE

JEREMIAH
PROPHET
UNDER
SIEGE

JAMES M. EFIRD

Judson Press ® Valley Forge

JEREMIAH—PROPHET UNDER SIEGE

Copyright © 1979
Judson Press, Valley Forge, PA 19481

Unless otherwise indicated, Bible quotations in this volume are in accordance with the Revised Standard Version of the Bible, copyrighted 1946, 1952, 1971, 1973 © by the Division of Christian Education of the National Council of the Churches of Christ in the United States of America, and are used by permission.

Library of Congress Cataloging in Publication Data

Efird, James M.
  Jeremiah, prophet under siege.

  Bibliography: p. 135
  1. Bible. O. T. Jeremiah—Criticism, interpretation,
etc. I. Title.
BS1525.2.E36   224′.2′06   79-14837
ISBN 0-8170-0846-2

For
MICHELLE
A Constant Joy

Preface

It was a distinct privilege for me to be asked by Harold L. Twiss, Managing Editor of Judson Press, to prepare a short book dealing with the life and teachings of the prophet Jeremiah. Of all the great prophets of Israel, Jeremiah stands out as one of the very greatest. We know more about his personal life than we do about any of the other prophets, and it may be that this is the reason why he becomes so real to those who study his ministry.

This book will attempt in a brief manner to examine the background for the study of the prophets, the specific circumstances in which Jeremiah performed his unique ministry, the elements of his personality that characterized Jeremiah the man, his relationship with his contemporaries, and the chief themes of his preaching ministry. A short concluding chapter will attempt to suggest ways in which the teachings of this great man of God can be applied to life in our contemporary society.

One major point should be stated clearly before turning to the man and his book. Far too often in the study of the books which Christians call the "Old Testament," the interpreter takes every occasion to relate the Old Testament teaching to the New Testament. Certainly for Christians this is not an illegitimate method of interpretation since the Christian church from its beginning has believed that the events depicted and presented in the New Testament writings were a direct outgrowth and, in a sense, fulfillment of the highest dreams and aspirations of the Old Testament writers. Too often, however, the books, especially the prophetic literature, are not examined in terms of their own time and place. By using this procedure the greatness and specificity of the Old Testament writings are simply overlooked. This happens to the detriment of our own study, for these books are also inspired messages of God for their generations. And if they contain truth, and we believe that they certainly do, it is incumbent upon us to examine these books very carefully to learn the truth contained therein! It is only after a thorough investigation to seek to learn the truth as it was delivered then that we can apply this truth to other contexts, i.e., the New Testament period and our own times.

The emphasis, then, in this short study guide will be focused upon the life and message of Jeremiah as it was directed toward and centered in his own time and place. There will be little reference to the way Jeremiah and his teachings have been interpreted by later Judaism or the early Christians. And it is hoped that this approach will open new possibilities for understanding not only Jeremiah but also other prophetic and Old Testament writings, for these are magnificent proclamations of the faith of those people who were called by God to reveal his message and himself to the people of that period—and ours.

The reader is advised here that the biblical text used is that of the Revised Standard Version. Whenever I deviate from that translation, the discussion will attempt to explain why that has been done. In addition to this, the term *Yahweh* will be used quite frequently as the personal name of the God of the Hebrew nations and of Jeremiah. The reader is urged to take note of how often it is used in the biblical text, for when that name underlies the English translation of the Revised Standard Version, the translators have given the readers a guide by printing either LORD or GOD in capital letters.

I would like to take this opportunity to thank a number of persons responsible for assisting in the completion of this work. My thanks are especially due Mr. Harold L. Twiss and his fine staff at Judson Press; my former teachers; those persons who have studied the prophetic literature with me over the years, both students in the Duke Divinity School and lay persons in numerous teaching assignments in churches; my colleague, Dr. Lloyd Bailey, who has made several helpful suggestions; and to my dear wife, Vivian, who has typed the manuscript and is always a constant source of strength for my life.

It is my hope that the study of the prophet Jeremiah will be an inspiration and a source of strength for all who undertake it.

Durham, North Carolina   *James M. Efird*

Contents

1
Background

Any study of the prophets or of a prophet must begin with at least a brief look at the nature of prophecy. The prophets and the books containing their messages are among the most misunderstood of all biblical literature; the only books which surpass them in this are those which fall into the literary category known as *apocalyptic* (i.e., The Book of Daniel and The Revelation to John). If anyone mentions the word "prophet" to us, the first concept which usually comes to mind is that of "predicting the future." But that is *our* way of understanding these people, not the way they understood themselves or were understood in their times.

The word used for prophet in the Hebrew of the Old Testament was *nabi'*. The origins of that word seem to be lost in the misty recesses of the past, but most scholars are agreed that the term comes from a basic root meaning "to call." The question arises at that point as to whether the word was understood in an active sense, i.e., to call out (to deliver a message), or in a passive sense, i.e., to be called (to be sent out to deliver a message). The latter interpretation is the most probable one, and it seems to fit the actual understanding of their mission and purpose as the prophets themselves understood it. They believed that Yahweh (the Hebrew personal name for God) had selected (called) them to deliver a message to the people.

The message which they were given was a message directed to the people of their own time and place. This is the reason one should always attempt to learn as much as one can about the historical situation which was extant at the time the prophet delivered his

13

message. It is true, however, that the prophets did at points look toward the future. But this was the future that was growing out of the present circumstances of that particular and specific time. Isaiah predicted, for example, that the nation of Judah would be delivered from two of its enemies (Syria and Israel) within two to twelve years (see Isaiah 7:10-17)—and it was! Jeremiah predicted that Judah would go into exile in Babylonia—and it did! He also predicted that the people would be there for a while before they would be allowed to return home—and they were.

In all of these illustrations (and many more could be cited) one notes that that which was predicted was for the *immediate* future, not the distant future. The prophet's first and foremost duty was to speak a word of God to the people then and there. Prediction is really only a secondary function and aspect of the prophetic office.

One of the reasons we have understood the prophets as "predictors" of the future is a result of the fact that the New Testament writers believed that the Old Testament was "fulfilled" in the events surrounding the life and ministry of Jesus and the development of the early church.

It is indeed true that the New Testament writers were convinced that these events did fulfill the teachings of the Old Testament. These understandings really have little to do with the interpretation of the Old Testament writings, but it is not out of place entirely to mention this problem briefly here. There are at least two points that need to be made. First, it must be realized that this fulfillment was not simply of the "predictions" of the prophets, but rather the fulfillment encompassed the full scope of the Old Testament writings. The recognition of this point leads to the second which must be kept in mind. The New Testament church basically interpreted "fulfillment" as more than a single "one to one" prediction and fulfillment on a literal plane. Rather the New Testament writers usually interpreted their Scriptures (i.e., the Old Testament) at a much deeper level. This was in line with the method of interpretation which Jesus himself emphasized in his own teaching. For example, in Matthew 5:17ff. there is a series of sayings which deals with the interpretation of the Scriptures. This list is called the "Antitheses" because the basic form of the sayings follows the pattern "You have heard it said, . . . but I say to you. . . ." The idea is that it is not enough simply, for example, to refrain from murder; one must not even hate or be angry with one's neighbor. (Other examples can be seen by reading the listing in

Matthew's Gospel.) The point is that the Scriptures are seen not as literal, face-value, externalistic commands or predictions, but rather as pointers to some greater religious or spiritual truth. In such an approach there may be some external resemblance to the literal meanings, but the essential message lies beneath that level of interpretation.

A very good example of this is found in the famous, well-known, and sometimes highly debated passage from Isaiah 7:14 quoted by Matthew in 1:23. In the original passage (Isaiah 7:10-17) the context and setting are that of a moment of history in which the two small kingdoms of Syria and Israel are poised to attack Judah. The king of Judah, Ahaz, was contemplating whether to appeal to the king of Assyria for assistance in meeting this threat. Isaiah was sent to Ahaz to urge that no appeal to Assyria be made, because this would make Judah a vassal of Assyria and meant that Judah would have to worship the gods of Assyria! Ahaz refused to listen to Isaiah, whereupon Isaiah told Ahaz that Yahweh would give him a sign. This sign would consist of a young woman (who was present at the time of this exchange and who was already pregnant and about ready to bear the child) having a child. And before that child was old enough to determine right from wrong (no less than two years nor more than twelve), the lands of Syria and Israel would be destroyed. Because of this Judah would be delivered from this threat; therefore the child would be called "Immanuel," which means in Hebrew "God is with us." This episode then is one which emphasizes *deliverance,* the deliverance of God's people from a very dangerous political and military threat. (Incidentally, this deliverance did in fact take place!)

Now when Matthew (or the early church) utilized this passage, the primary emphasis was not upon the idea of the "virgin." This is not to deny that Matthew knew the tradition of the virgin birth and definitely taught it. But it is to say that if this is the only idea one finds in Matthew's use of the Isaiah passage, the more important and much more significant point is missed. The author of the Gospel of Matthew wished to emphasize the deeper meaning of the text, the idea of deliverance. In this case, however, it is not a deliverance from a political or military threat to one particular country but deliverance from a much more vicious enemy of the entire human race. The deliverance here is deliverance from sin which enslaves the world and the people of the world. It is, therefore, at this deeper level that Matthew intended the passage to be understood. If one could diagram the idea involved here, it would look something like this.

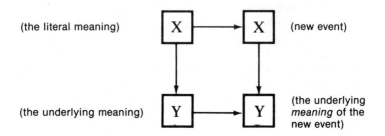

(the literal meaning)   X ⟶ X   (new event)

(the underlying meaning)   Y ⟶ Y   (the underlying *meaning* of the new event)

It is at the "Y" level that the significant "fulfillment" takes place. Deliverance from sin means in truth that God is with us!

Far too many persons have gone astray in interpreting the fulfillment of the Old Testament in general and the prophets in particular in the events of the New Testament by emphasizing only the "X" level. In reality that level is at best secondary to the real essence of the situation, and at times not even relevant! But by concentrating on this "X" level, the misunderstanding of prophecy as basically "prediction" has been enhanced and perpetuated.

To understand prophecy, therefore, one must put aside the idea that prophets were primarily predictors of the future. The prophet of the Old Testament basically had two characteristics: (1) he was called by Yahweh; and (2) he was to proclaim the message of Yahweh to the people. The prophets were then historically conditioned and must be understood against the background of their own particular historical situation. It was to that specific context that the prophet spoke. What prediction there was arose out of that immediate context and related to the *immediate,* not the long-range, future. In short, the prophet was one who spoke the words of God to the people of his time.

The specific historical context in which the prophetic movement developed (from the ninth through the fifth centuries B.C.) was that of the political statehood of Israel and Judah. Beginning with the figure of Elijah, the prophet more and more became a solitary figure who spoke God's message to king, priest, people, and sometimes even other prophets! When the end of that era of Israelite history was concluded, other instruments were used by God to speak to the needs of the people. Thus the prophetic movement as such faded and gave way to the other movements of wisdom and apocalyptic in the later postexilic period of Israelite history (i.e., after *ca.* 500 B.C.).

Scholars have argued about exactly how the prophetic movement began and developed in Israel, and no one theory does justice to all the aspects involved. It does not really serve the purpose here to enter into a long discussion of this matter. Suffice it to say that many tributaries fed into the mainstream which eventually became the prophetic movement.

It is well to discuss one aspect concerning the interpretation of the prophets which has been debated by the learned for some time now. This involves the difference between preexilic prophecy and postexilic prophecy. Since the prophets spoke to specific historical situations, it is clear that the message to be delivered to one context would probably be different from the message to be delivered to another context. And further, since the context of the preexilic period was quite different from that of the postexilic period, it is reasonable to assume that the messages of the prophets in each of these contexts would be different from one another.

Older scholarship, therefore, found the difference in the two eras as that between "doom" and "hope." Since the preexilic prophets were speaking to a people who were breaking the precepts of the covenant made between God and themselves, and since they seemed to be ignoring the warnings of the prophets and getting more obtuse rather than repenting of their evil ways, the message to this group was a message of doom. Yahweh would punish them for their sins, for turning their backs upon him, for refusing to be willing to repent. When the judgment did in fact come (in 721 B.C. to the Northern Kingdom of Israel, in 597–586 B.C. to the Southern Kingdom of Judah), the historical context no longer called for doom but for hope.

In general, this scheme is quite logical and correct. What happened, however, was a hardening of these guidelines to the point that any hope passage found in a preexilic prophetic book was automatically denied to the preexilic prophet. The hope passage was understood to be a later addition to the sayings of that prophet from the postexilic times. The reason that so many such sayings found their way into the collection of the preexilic prophetic oracles was a result of the fact that the sayings of the prophets were at first preserved orally, passed down by word of mouth from generation to generation, until they were finally written down and collected into a "book" sometime in the postexilic period. In such a "free-floating" method of remembering and preserving the teachings of these great personages, it would not be surprising to find that later hopes and ideas would occasionally find their way into the more harsh proclamations of the preexilic prophets. Thus it could be explained quite easily how and why there were hope sayings in the preexilic prophetic books. Thus the argument ran.

At the present time, however, scholars are not quite so rigid in their approach to the material. Each saying containing hope is examined, and a decision is made individually as to whether the passage is authentic in terms of coming from the preexilic prophet. This discussion is important because so much writing on the prophets has come from or been under the influence of that basic understanding. One should be aware of such presuppositions. Secondly, the problem is acutely felt in dealing with the prophet Jeremiah. This man's career lasted for a long period of time (possibly 626–581 B.C.) and came at the moment in time which preceded, coincided with, and followed the destruction and exile of Judah and its people. The historical context of Jeremiah's time is crucial to understanding the man and his message.

Historical Summary of Jeremiah's Time

In order to understand Jeremiah and his teaching, it is essential to give a brief summary of the historical period into which he came and to which he delivered his message. The Northern Kingdom had fallen in 721 B.C. to the mighty Assyrian army; the people had been taken away; and foreigners had been brought in to repopulate the land. Israel did not return from its exile.

About the same time in Judah a good king, Hezekiah, came to the throne. He instituted religious reforms; to do this in those days was an act of rebellion against the nation with which one was allied, in this case, Assyria. The king of Assyria came into the land capturing almost all of the fortified cities and ravaging the entire countryside. Sennacherib, the Assyrian king, then besieged the city of Jerusalem itself, but Isaiah told Hezekiah not to relent, that Jerusalem would not be taken. And it was not. Sennacherib left to return to his own country. Whether this was because of pressing matters at home or whether a plague decimated the army is not known. Herodotus, the Greek historian, mentions this incident in his history saying that the rats ate the bowstrings of the Assyrians! This mention of rats may well reflect that a plague did indeed spread through the army. The biblical writers interpreted this, as one would expect, as the hand of

God delivering his city from the pagans. To the Assyrians the taking of Jerusalem was not all that important since they had captured almost all of the land and its cities and had won large concessions from Hezekiah otherwise. This incident, however, led the people to believe that Yahweh would not allow anyone at any time to harm Jerusalem, an idea that Jeremiah would eventually have to deal with.

After Hezekiah came Manasseh, the worst king Judah ever had according to the writers of the books of Kings. He reigned, however, longer than any other king of Judah! During his reign all sorts of pagan deities were worshiped; a general moral decay among the people continued and grew worse; and even the horrible rite of child sacrifice was practiced. It is also quite probable that the prophets were persecuted, since we hear no prophetic voice from this time.

Shortly after the death of Manasseh in 642 B.C., his son, Josiah, became king. At this time he was only eight years old (640 B.C.). During Josiah's reign (ca. 622 B.C.) there was found in the temple (which was being repaired) a "book of the law" (see 2 Kings 22). The document was ultimately brought to Josiah and read to him. The contents of this book so moved Josiah that he instituted a sweeping reform movement in Judah known as the "Deuteronomic" reform. The name comes from the fact that the aspects of the reform as it is described in Second Kings are found in Deuteronomy, especially chapters 12–26 and 28.

Simply put, the reform banned all foreign cults and worship, forbade child sacrifice, and, most importantly, centered all worship in the Jerusalem temple. The shrines at outlying places were banned. This necessitated a new arrangement for the priests so that none would be displaced because of the reform. They were to come to Jerusalem to officiate at the temple at certain times during the year on a rotating basis. The importance of the reform in general and of the centralization of worship in the temple in particular cannot be emphasized too strongly in relation to Jeremiah.

Josiah's reform was assisted greatly, politically speaking, by the decline of the Assyrian empire. It was soon after, in 612 B.C., that the capital of that great empire, Nineveh, fell to the Babylonians. Even though Assyria was defeated, some elements of the army continued to fight. And to the assistance of that element Egypt sent troops. It was not that Egypt liked Assyria; far from it. But Egypt saw that a strong Babylonian kingdom would be a threat. Therefore, troops were sent to assist the Assyrians.

During this period Josiah was loosely allied with the Babyloni-ans. When the Egyptians sent aid, Josiah went out to meet them to keep them from joining the Assyrian army. There was a battle at Megiddo where Josiah was killed (609 B.C.). The Egyptians, therefore, placed upon the throne of Judah a son of Josiah who was pro-Egyptian and who was in essence a vassal of Egypt. His name was Jehoiakim (who was not next in line to be king). With the advent of this man to the throne, the Deuteronomic reform movement was dead. Pagan cults were reintroduced into the land. The moral fiber of the leaders and the people completely collapsed.

There was, however, a great deal of optimism among the people. Taking the idea of the inviolability of Jerusalem from Isaiah and coupling it with the centralization of all legitimate worship in Jerusalem, the people believed that Yahweh would not allow any evil to befall his city and his place (i.e., the temple). They felt secure, so secure that they were convinced that no matter what *they* did, Yahweh would protect them because they were part of his city and dwelling place.

After the death of Josiah in 609 B.C. the Egyptians moved on to fight against the Babylonians. Even though they were not successful in defeating them, the Egyptians were able to keep them from coming any farther into Palestine. Judah remained a vassal state of Egypt until 605 B.C. In that year the Babylonians soundly defeated the Egyptians at Carchemish (a city far north of Judah near the old Assyrian Empire) and swept down into Palestine itself. In 604 B.C. Jehoiakim became a vassal of Nebuchadnezzar, the famous Baby-lonian leader.

Jehoiakim, however, remained an Egyptian sympathizer, and, encouraged by a brief Babylonian withdrawal from the frontier (ca. 600 B.C.), he rebelled. It took the Babylonians a short while to mobilize in order to move against Judah. In late 598 their army came into the land. Jehoiakim died at that very time, whether of natural causes or otherwise is not known. His son, Jehoiachin, was placed on the throne. It fell to him to have to surrender to the Babylonians. Nebuchadnezzar deported the king and numerous court officials and others to Babylon. He allowed Judah to remain in existence, however, and placed Zedekiah (one of Josiah's sons) on the throne (see 2 Kings 24).

Even though a considerable number of leaders had been deported in 597, a large number of "lesser lights" were left to help guide the country in its attempt to survive. The king, Zedekiah, was a weak personality. He vacillated between doing what was right for the country and what his more militant pro-Egyptian advisers counseled. Naturally the Egyptians encouraged all the rebellion against Babylonia that they could among the smaller nations lying between Egypt and Babylonia.

This situation was intensified in 594–593 B.C. when it appeared to the people in Palestine that Babylonia was having troubles. A number of smaller nations along with Judah gathered to discuss plans for a possible rebellion. For whatever reasons that conference came to naught. But in 589 rebellion broke out again. Spurred by possible promises of aid from Egypt and by a group of enthusiastic nobles and prophets assuring a victory by Yahweh over the forces of Babylonia, Judah rebelled. It was a fatal mistake.

The Babylonian army moved into the area, and by mid-summer of 587 Jerusalem fell to the invaders. Zedekiah attempted to escape but was captured. He was forced to witness the execution of his children, whereupon he was immediately blinded. He was taken captive to Babylon and died there. Nebuchadnezzar ordered that Jerusalem be burned and its walls torn down. Many persons were simply executed, and many others were deported to Babylon. There were very few people left in the land, and they were basically the poor and uneducated.

At this time Nebuchadnezzar organized the area as a province within his empire and appointed a certain Gedaliah as governor over the area. After a short period, however, Gedaliah was murdered by a subversive group headed by a man named Ishmael. The people around Gedaliah fled to Egypt; Ishmael fled to the land of Ammon. It is possible but not provable that Nebuchadnezzar ordered another deportation in 582–581 B.C. This is far from certain, however. At this point Judah became part of the province of Samaria. As far as political history is concerned, Judah does not reappear for some time. And even when the exiles (or some of them) returned to the land from Babylonia (538 B.C. ff.), there was really no significant political entity here until the time of the Maccabean era, i.e., after 165 B.C.

It was into this political and cultural arena that Jeremiah came with his messages from Yahweh.

The Book of Jeremiah: Critical Issues

The most difficult problem encountered in dealing with the

Book of Jeremiah (or almost any other prophetic book, for that matter) is that of how the book came to be in its present form. This question is not simply of historical interest, but it is a pressing concern for anyone who wishes to study the teachings of the prophet. Is the book in any kind of order? If so, what kind? Does the material seem to be all of one type, or are there several types of literary forms contained within the collection? These questions and many more are important because they affect to a great extent how one approaches and interprets the material incorporated within the book.

The reason for the problem at this point relates to and evolves from the fact that the prophets were basically speakers, not writers. Even though older commentators often referred to the classical prophets as "writing" prophets, it is almost universally agreed today that this was not the case. The sayings of the great prophets were remembered and transmitted orally at first, until such a time as they began to be collected together into sayings "groups" and finally arranged together in the form in which we have them now. The process or processes which were involved in producing these books cannot be precisely recovered. Any suggestion as to what happened, when, or by whom is simply that—a suggestion or a conjectural hypothesis.

Another factor that should be discussed somewhere, and here is perhaps as good a place as any, concerns the mode of expression utilized by the prophets. The basic point to be remembered when reading the prophetic sayings (usually called "oracles") is that they were primarily spoken in *poetic* form. This is an important factor, for one must always recall that poetry is not the same as prose nor is it intended to be understood exactly as prose. The poet must be allowed the so-called "poetic license," the freedom to express thoughts by exaggerated or symbolic language. Anyone who has studied poetry knows that the poetic expressions are quite often not intended to be interpreted literally but point beyond the mere words to a deeper meaning and intent which the poet is attempting to convey to the hearers or readers.

It is also necessary for the reader or student of the prophetic literature to have some idea about the characteristics of Hebrew poetry. Contrary to our usual understanding of poetic characteristics, which ordinarily include rhyme and rhythm, Hebrew poetry is distinguished by something entirely different. This is not to say that rhyme and/or rhythm were not a part of Hebrew poetry, for at times they definitely were, but the basic characteristic of Hebrew poetry lies in a phenomenon known as "parallelism."

This feature of Hebrew poetry can best be understood in its simplest form as a two-line structure of thought. The first line makes a statement; the second line then relates to that statement in one of three ways. First, the second line simply repeats the meaning of the first line. This is called synonymous parallelism. Some examples of it are:

> Deliver me from my enemies, O my God,
>> protect me from those who rise up against me,
>>> —Psalm 59:1

> "Why did I not die at birth,
>> come forth from the womb and expire?"
>>> —Job 3:11

> My son, do not despise the LORD's discipline
>> or be weary of his reproof,
>>> —Proverbs 3:11

> For the needy shall not always be forgotten,
>> and the hope of the poor shall not perish for ever.
>>> —Psalm 9:18

In the second type of parallelism, the second line makes a statement that is the opposite of, or contradictory to, that of the first line. This is called antithetical parallelism. Some examples of this type are:

> A soft answer turns away wrath,
>> but a harsh word stirs up anger.
>>> —Proverbs 15:1

> Better is a dry morsel with quiet
>> than a house full of feasting with strife.
>>> —Proverbs 17:1

> for the LORD knows the way of the righteous,
>> but the way of the wicked will perish.
>>> —Psalm 1:6

> O let the evil of the wicked come to an end,
>> but establish thou the righteous.
>>> —Psalm 7:9a

In the third type of parallelism the second line makes a statement that explains or expands or builds upon the meaning of the first line. This is called synthetic parallelism. Some examples of this type are:

> I will give thanks to the LORD with my whole heart;
> I will tell of all thy wonderful deeds.
>> —Psalm 9:1

> I sought the LORD, and he answered me,
> and delivered me from all my fears.
>> —Psalm 34:4

> "Behold, happy is the man whom God reproves;
> therefore despise not the chastening of the Almighty."
>> —Job 5:17

> Go to the ant, O sluggard;
> consider her ways, and be wise.
>> —Proverbs 6:6

While there are refinements and expansions on these basic types, one can easily recognize these when they occur. The primary point to keep in mind is that the bulk of the prophetic teachings is conveyed in poetic form.

Another problem which arises in studying the prophetic books has to do with the way the books were finally edited and placed together. There seems to be a set pattern for the three major prophetic works, namely Isaiah (chapters 1–39), Jeremiah, and Ezekiel. Each of these was at one time or another divided into three basic sections. The first contained a series of oracles by the prophet dealing with the nation Judah. This was followed by a section containing oracles against foreign nations. The third portion contained oracles of hope for the future. In both Isaiah and Jeremiah there was also a historical section reciting some incident in the history of that time. Those historical summaries roughly paralleled sections of the historical work, Second Kings.

It is not the purpose here to investigate these matters fully, but only to make the reader aware that these kinds of patterns were used by the editors and compilers of these books. What is important to note is that the Book of Jeremiah, as we have it today, was at one time arranged in such a pattern. The first section of the book, 1:1–25:13, contained primarily oracles against Judah. We know from the Greek translation of the Old Testament (called the Septuagint) that what we now have as chapters 46–51 (a collection of oracles against foreign nations) was at one time found after 25:13*a*. They were also in a different order. Since the Septuagint translation of the prophetic books was not made until the second century B.C., the order of the Hebrew text was not fixed until later. It is also interesting to note that the Greek text of Jeremiah is approximately one-eighth shorter than the Hebrew text with which most of us are familiar.

The point of discussing such a technical matter is simply to alert the student of Jeremiah in particular (and of all the prophetic books in general) to the fact that the text of the book and how it was put together in the form we now have were the result of complicated processes. To ascertain exactly how any one of the prophetic books came to be in its present form is a difficult task. That task is even more difficult with Jeremiah because we know more about certain events in his life that relate to the preservation of his teachings than about those in the life of any other prophet.

Almost all studies of the Book of Jeremiah begin with a reference to an incident recorded for us in chapter 36. In 605 B.C. Jeremiah dictated to his trusted friend and scribe, Baruch, a series of oracles (supposedly delivered over the years) against the land. As Jeremiah had requested, Baruch took the scroll to the temple to read it aloud, publicly, there. Some of the princes of the government were summoned to hear the scroll read. Baruch then read the scroll to them.

These princes took the scroll, ordered Baruch to find Jeremiah and for both of them to hide, and reported what had happened to the king. Whether they did this because they were sympathetic with Jeremiah's message or they felt this was the safest and easiest method to get the scroll out of public circulation and win themselves approval with the king is not known. We know that they reported the incident to King Jehoiakim. He had the scroll brought to him and read. Upon hearing several columns, he took a penknife, cut off what had been read, and then dropped the document piece by piece into the fire. When he had burned it all, he ordered that Jeremiah and Baruch both be arrested.

Later Jeremiah dictated another scroll to Baruch and even added many other words of the "same type." The importance of this episode preserved for us in Jeremiah 36 is perhaps two-fold: first it is significant that a prophet in his own lifetime had his oracles put into writing; and further it is possible that this scroll became the foundation document or collection for the compilation of the Book of Jeremiah as we have it. Since most of the oracles contained in chapters 1–25 seem to come from the era before 605 B.C., there are numerous scholars who argue that these chapters formed the basic content of that scroll dictated to Baruch. Whether that conjecture is true cannot be proved, but it is true that these chapters do seem to form one collection of Jeremianic material used as a basic element in the structuring of this book.

In addition to this basic collection of the oracles of Jeremiah in chapters 1–25 there were numerous other collections of material which are found within the book as it has been preserved for us. A second collection, for example, is reflected in the sayings against foreign nations found in our Bibles in chapters 46–51. As already indicated, these chapters at one time were found after 25:13a. In this collection are genuine proclamations of Jeremiah, but many scholars think that a few of these oracles were added later to the original older collection which came from Jeremiah himself.

A third element in the compilation of the book can be discerned in chapters 30–31, possibly even 30–33. These sayings and events deal primarily with hope; therefore some commentators call these the "Book of Consolation." Whether these chapters were originally one collection, or whether 30–31 and 32–33 were originally separate and later placed together by editors and redactors, we do not know for certain. But they are linked together by a common theme, hope.

Another possible source may be found in the materials primarily located in chapters 26–29 and 34–45. These stories are basically biographical prose accounts dealing with episodes in the life of Jeremiah. Some scholars call the one or ones who compiled these accounts the "biographer" of Jeremiah. The identity of the person who collected and wrote down these episodes is not known, but many think (and that is as good a guess as any) that Jeremiah's trusted friend, Baruch, was responsible for these accounts (or most of them). It is, however, probably too much to call this collection a "biography" of the great prophet. The incidents are separate and not arranged in any kind of chronological order at all. The best guess is that these stories dealing with typical incidents in the life of Jeremiah were collected together and edited in the exilic period *(ca.* 550 B.C.). This was done by a group of people known as the Deuteronomic editors because their theology and style reflect that of the book of

Deuteronomy. They also edited a basic survey of the history of Israel which encompassed the books of Deuteronomy, Joshua, Judges, First and Second Samuel, First and Second Kings.

Finally, there is the historical chapter (52) which was added to complete the collection as it is now known to us. Exactly how these various collections came into existence and how they were then combined into the Book of Jeremiah as we now have it are simply not discernible to us. But the fact that so much was remembered and preserved about the life and teachings of Jeremiah shows the esteem in which later generations held this great prophet. Unfortunately for him (and for them), that esteem was withheld by his own generation. His was a lonely life and a difficult ministry, but Jeremiah's commitment and efforts have meant much to persons who through the centuries have valued his teachings and example.

2
Jeremiah, the Man

Even though a great deal is known about Jeremiah's life as a prophetic messenger of God, very little is known about his background. We are told at the beginning of the book that he was "... the son of Hilkiah, of the priests who were in Anathoth in the land of Benjamin" (1:1). Anathoth was a small town about three or four miles northeast of Jerusalem in the old territory of northern Israel! This may explain Jeremiah's interest in and obvious affection for the people of the then exiled Northern Kingdom and for the traditions which have been associated with the Northern Kingdom— that of Deuteronomy and Hosea, the one true northern prophet.

His family was of priestly descent but in all probability was not connected with the trappings of the Jerusalem temple. Many interpreters of the Old Testament connect Jeremiah's family with the priest Abiathar who was exiled to Anathoth when Solomon became king upon David's death. Abiathar had been the priest during David's reign, but he championed David's elder son (Adonijah) for the kingship. When Solomon won that power struggle, however, Abiathar was expelled from the land. As a member of a priestly family, Jeremiah would probably have had access to religious traditions usually unknown to ordinary people. And he does seem to have been exposed to various traditions, especially those relating to Samuel and the Ark of the Covenant. One recalls that early in Israel's history this ark was considered to be the most important cultic possession which Israel had. But the basic fact is that we know little about Jeremiah's family, his youth, or his education.

What we are told is that in the thirteenth year of the reign of King Josiah, Jeremiah was called to be a prophet. This date would be 627–626 B.C. Some scholars find difficulties with this date, however, since one is very hard pressed to find any oracles of Jeremiah that seem to fit the years 626–609 B.C. (One recalls that it was in 609 that Josiah was killed and Jehoiakim was placed on the throne by the Egyptians.) And further, there are very few, if any, allusions to Josiah's reform with which Jeremiah would have in all probability been in agreement. There is a reference or so to Josiah, and these references present Josiah as admired and respected by Jeremiah but no longer alive. Therefore, it is curious that so little reference is made to the period 626–609, and what there is seems to be very uncertain.

This set of circumstances has led some more recent scholars and interpreters of Jeremiah to argue that Jeremiah was not "called" in 626 to begin his prophetic ministry actively, but that this date should be interpreted as the date of Jeremiah's birth. Since Jeremiah interpreted his call to be a prophet to have been given while he was "still in the womb" (1:5), this would make sense of all the data. Jeremiah was called to be a prophet from his conception, but his public ministry only began after Jehoiakim began to reign as king over Judah (ca. 609 B.C.). That would make him about seventeen or eighteen years old when he began his ministry. This also helps to explain his reluctance to become a prophet at such an early age, for youth was not valued very highly by persons in that culture. They felt that respect and wisdom came with length of years. A young man proclaiming to the nation a message of repentance and doom would not be well received—and Jeremiah knew that.

Even though we do have numerous incidents from the life of Jeremiah recorded in the book bearing his name, we nevertheless do not have enough data to write anything like a biography of his ministry. We do know that his life was one of loneliness and conflict with the political and religious leaders. On several occasions he was extremely close to being put to death (see 26:16ff.; 37–38). In one of his confessions he himself seems to refer to a plot against his life (11:18ff.). His countrymen considered him a traitor, but it is difficult to find another prophet who seemed to love his country and his people so deeply in spite of their unworthiness.

Much more could be said about the background for Jeremiah's ministry, but it is more important perhaps to move as quickly as possible into the basic elements of his message. It is in order, however, to mention one further point as part of the background for understanding his ministry. This point has to do with Jeremiah's first public proclamation during the reign of Jehoiakim. If this is the beginning of his ministry, it may well be the first public proclamation of his entire career.

This event took place at the gate of the temple and is recorded in two different places in the Book of Jeremiah, attesting to its significance in the life of Jeremiah (chapters 7, 26). We remember that, in the aftermath of Isaiah's word to Hezekiah (*ca.* 701 B.C.) that Sennacherib (the Assyrian king) would not capture Jerusalem, many felt Jerusalem was inviolate. Yahweh would protect his city against all threats, no matter what the condition of Yahweh's people. This kind of thinking was given additional impetus through the Deuteronomic reform instituted by Josiah in 621. Since all worship was now centered in the temple in Jerusalem, this had the effect of making the people even more certain that Yahweh would never allow his city to be captured or destroyed.

Even though Jeremiah probably approved of the reform under Josiah, we have no oracle from him that specifically relates to that time period. He does speak very approvingly of Josiah, but these comments are made with reference to the past after Josiah had died. When Jehoiakim became king, it was soon obvious that the reform movement had lost any real substance which it may have at one time had. The king allowed all sorts of pagan practices to be reinstituted and was concerned very little about the moral well-being of the people.

The people, however, still held to their two-fold hope of the inviolability of Jerusalem and the presence of the temple there. In fact, the city and the temple had become talismans which ensured their protection and security. To that kind of situation Jeremiah was called to speak in the name of Yahweh. The temple "sermon" was a blistering denunciation of the religious and moral life-style of the people. There are two accounts of this event, one found in the "teachings" section of Jeremiah (7:1-15) and one in the "biographical" section (26:1-9). The latter account seems to be the one nearest to the original, for the account in chapter 7 has had some additional teachings added to it (see 36:32). It would be well to cite the teachings directed to the people.

The word that came to Jeremiah from the LORD: "Stand in the

gate of the LORD'S house, and proclaim there this word, and say, Hear the word of the LORD, all you men of Judah who enter these gates to worship the LORD. Thus says the LORD of hosts, the God of Israel, Amend your ways and your doings, and I will let you dwell in this place. Do not trust in these deceptive words: 'This is the temple of the LORD, the temple of the LORD, the temple of the LORD.'

"For if you truly amend your ways and your doings, if you truly execute justice one with another, if you do not oppress the alien, the fatherless or the widow, or shed innocent blood in this place, and if you do not go after other gods to your own hurt, then I will let you dwell in this place, in the land that I gave of old to your fathers for ever.

"Behold, you trust in deceptive words to no avail. Will you steal, murder, commit adultery, swear falsely, burn incense to Baal, and go after other gods that you have not known, and then come and stand before me in this house, which is called by my name, and say, 'We are delivered!'—only to go on doing all these abominations? Has this house, which is called by my name, become a den of robbers in your eyes? Behold, I myself have seen it, says the LORD. Go now to my place that was in Shiloh, where I made my name dwell at first, and see what I did to it for the wickedness of my people Israel. And now, because you have done all these things, says the LORD, and when I spoke to you persistently you did not listen, and when I called you, you did not answer, therefore I will do to the house which is called by my name, and in which you trust, and to the place which I gave to you and to your fathers, as I did to Shiloh. And I will cast you out of my sight, as I cast out all your kinsmen, all the offspring of Ephraim" (7:1-15).

One can well imagine the impact of this message on the people. There was so much hostility aroused that the account in chapter 26 adds an additional incident to the teachings. Jeremiah was tried on a charge of treason (26:10ff.). It is very interesting to note that the accusers in this incident were the priests and the prophets, the religious leaders who should have been the most sensitive to what Jeremiah was saying. Were it not for the "princes and the people" who argued that Jeremiah should not be killed for speaking in the name of Yahweh, he may well have been put to death. They referred to the prophecy of Micah which stated that Zion would be plowed "as a field" (see Jeremiah 26:18; Micah 3:12). Their argument was that this harsh statement by Micah helped to bring about the reform under King Hezekiah which led to the deliverance of the city.

In this discussion they referred also to another prophet, Uriah, who had prophesied similar words not long before. He had fled to Egypt to avoid the wrath of Jehoiakim, but Jehoiakim's men found him and returned him to Judah. Whereupon Jehoiakim promptly killed him. This additional information is included at this point to emphasize that Jeremiah's life was in *real* danger. Jeremiah was also assisted by a certain Ahikam whose family was part of the political structure of that time. Ahikam himself had been some kind of official under King Josiah (see 2 Kings 22:12, 14) and was in all probability sensitive to the message which Jeremiah had brought to the nation under its new king who was very unlike Josiah.

The temple sermon itself was very clear. The people could not substitute the *presence* of the temple (and in all probability the cultic sacrifices and ritual) for real religious commitment. What Yahweh required was a relationship with himself that transformed people. The old ways could no longer be tolerated; old morals were not acceptable.

"Will you steal, murder, commit adultery, swear falsely, burn incense to Baal, and go after other gods that you have not known, and then come and stand before me in this house, which is called by my name, and say, 'We are delivered!'—only to go on doing all these abominations?" (7:9-10).

This is sheer hypocrisy. And hypocrisy, especially in religious matters, is always rewarded by punishment. To bolster his argument, Jeremiah referred to the old traditions associated with Shiloh. This was the site where early in Israel's history the religious center of the people was situated. It was the home for the Ark of the Covenant, *the* significant cultic adornment of the Hebrew people where Yahweh's presence was supposed to reside. All these ideas had now been transferred to the Jerusalem temple. But because of the sin of the people of Israel, Shiloh was destroyed and the ark was captured (see 1 Samuel 4–6). That took place at about 1050 B.C. The shrine had not yet been restored or rebuilt even till the time of Jeremiah! If indeed Yahweh could once do that to the place of his presence because of the sin of the people, he could certainly do it again. For to Jeremiah the

sin of his time was just as heinous, in fact more so, as the sin of the
people of that era.

The stage was therefore set for Jeremiah's ministry. Jeremiah,
almost alone, against the people, the king, and the religious leaders—
both priests and prophets—was to have a long and bitter service to a
people who did not appreciate him or understand the message which
he had to deliver to them.

Jeremiah's Call to Become a Prophet

The words of Jeremiah, the son of Hilkiah, of the priests who
were in Anathoth in the land of Benjamin, to whom the word of the
LORD came in the days of Josiah the son of Amon, king of Judah, in
the thirteenth year of his reign. It came also in the days of
Jehoiakim the son of Josiah, king of Judah, and until the end of the
eleventh year of Zedekiah, the son of Josiah, king of Judah, until
the captivity of Jerusalem in the fifth month (1:1-3).

We have already discussed the problem of the date of Jeremiah's
call. If the text in 1:2 is to be taken as the time Jeremiah's prophetic
call and ministry began, that would have been 627–626 B.C. As noted,
the difficulty with this position is that there are so few oracles from
Jeremiah that can be designated with any confidence as having come
from the period 626–609 B.C. And further, Jeremiah never specifically
mentioned the Deuteronomic reform put into effect by Josiah with
which one assumes he would have been at least partially in
agreement. Most of his teaching relates specifically to the period of
Judah's history which began with the reign of King Jehoiakim.
Therefore, the position taken here is that Jeremiah began his public
ministry in 609 B.C.; the date given then in 1:2 is the date of his birth.
And some evidence for that can be seen in the fact that Jeremiah
understood his call from God to be a prophet to have been given while
he was still in his mother's womb!

> Now the word of the LORD came to me saying,
> "Before I formed you in the womb
>   I knew you,
> and before you were born I consecrated you;
>   I appointed you a prophet to the nations."

Then I said, "Ah, Lord GOD! Behold, I do not know how to speak,
for I am only a youth." But the LORD said to me,

> "Do not say, 'I am only a youth';
> for to all to whom I send you you shall go,
> and whatever I command you you shall speak.
> Be not afraid of them,
> for I am with you to deliver you,
>   says the LORD."
>   Then the LORD put forth his hand and touched my mouth; and
> the LORD said to me,
> "Behold, I have put my words in your mouth.
> See, I have set you this day over nations and over kingdoms,
> to pluck up and to break down,
> to destroy and to overthrow,
> to build and to plant."
>
> —Jeremiah 1:4-10

One of the chief characteristics of the Hebrew prophets was a conviction that Yahweh had *called* them to be his spokespersons. Not all the prophetic books describe in full a call experience like that of Isaiah (Isaiah 6:1-13) or Ezekiel (Ezekiel, chapters 1-2), but most of the prophets were acutely aware that they had been especially singled out as persons who were to speak for God to his people. Jeremiah no less than the others felt this special call.

Jeremiah's call, as it is recorded for us in these verses, evidently did not come in the form of a dramatic vision. The text simply says that the word of Yahweh came to him. But what a word it turned out to be! Yahweh told Jeremiah that before he was formed in the womb, he had already been selected to be a prophet to the nations. There are some very significant points which deserve to be mentioned in connection with verse 5.

First of all, the meaning of the Hebrew verbs translated "knew" and "consecrated" is crucial to an understanding of this episode in Jeremiah's life. The verb "to know" in the Old Testament has a much broader and richer meaning than simply intellectual knowledge. The term is as much one designating relationship as anything else. And the relationship is one of an intimate type.

Another dimension in this word (related to the verb "consecrated" in the second line of the verse) is that of "selection," usually for a specific purpose. The term quite frequently contains the idea ordinarily known as "election." This concept is an exceedingly important one in the biblical writings. It designates that Yahweh has called someone to perform a certain task for him. Abraham was elected to be a means whereby all the nations of the earth might be blessed (see Genesis 12:2-3). Moses was selected to lead the Hebrew people out of Egypt for a purpose, so that Yahweh's name might be made great in all the world (see Exodus 9:15-16). The prophets were called, "elected," to speak God's word and message to the people of God.

Quite frequently in present-day thinking election is thought of as synonymous with salvation. But that is a modern idea. To the biblical writers (both of the Old and New Testaments) election was more important and took precedence over the idea of salvation. The two are not identical in meaning. Election is always God's selection of someone to perform a certain task. Salvation is a form of deliverance, God's intervention on behalf of his people. But the most important and significant of these was election; to be chosen as a special worker for God was an honor indeed.

The word translated "consecrated" is closely related in meaning to the idea of election. The word means "set apart," usually set apart for a mission on behalf of Yahweh. Jeremiah's work was to be a prophet to the nations! It was staggering enough to the young man to be called to preach Yahweh's word to the people of Judah, but Jeremiah was called to expand his horizons, to understand something more about the nature and activity of Yahweh, that this God was not limited by time or geographical locale or even by being associated closely with a specific people. This God was a God of the nations, who were used by him to accomplish his goals and will in and through the historical process. As Jeremiah's understanding of God expanded, so did his responsibilities to that God! He learned early that Yahweh was larger than he had ever dreamed! Therefore, his duties and responsibilities were similarly enlarged.

As did other prophets, Jeremiah felt a distinct unworthiness to undertake this massive task. Humanly speaking it was beyond him. Moses himself had also attempted to shrink from his election (see Exodus 4:1-17); Isaiah had cried out that he was a man of unclean lips and dwelt in the midst of a people of unclean lips (Isaiah 6:5); Amos had declared that he was not a prophet, but Yahweh spoke to him and he became a prophet (see Amos 7:14-15; 3:8b). The examples could be continued, but the point is clear. The prophets did not feel worthy to perform their tasks; the job was too great for them as mere mortals to attempt.

But as with all these men elected by God to proclaim his message, Jeremiah was given the promise that Yahweh would be with him. The young lad was not to shrink from the task simply because he was young, or because he was afraid. God promised to be with him, to give him the message, and to protect him from his foes—of which there were to be many.

Yahweh then touched Jeremiah's mouth (see Isaiah 6:6-7) and told him what kind of message he would be called upon to speak. Perhaps it would be appropriate at this point to make the observation that a spoken word in that time was not considered to be an empty breeze. That age considered that words had a certain power in and of themselves to bring about the meaning incorporated within the words. This is a somewhat new idea to us who are constantly inundated with a sea of words which have very little meaning in terms of actual accomplishment. But to that society words were not to be used lightly. This is the reason one finds in the Old Testament especially strict rules governing blessings and curses, and why it was considered such a dangerous thing to use the name of God in anything other than the most serious manner.

Therefore, when prophets were called upon by Yahweh to deliver his word to the people, that meant much more to them than simply a recitation of empty words. It meant to them that they were actually participants in the acts of God, for the words had power in themselves to accomplish the meaning inherent within them. This is also why the people hated the prophets so much when they brought messages of doom and destruction. It was their belief that the fact of the words being uttered against the nation was an act of treason not to be taken lightly. One can recall several incidents where that understanding is clearly portrayed (see Jeremiah's famous temple sermon, already discussed, and also Amos's words against the land of Israel, Amos 7:10-13).

Jeremiah was called to this task which, humanly speaking, was more than he could do. But whereas most of the earlier prophets had proclaimed a basic message of Yahweh's judgment on the sinful nation, Jeremiah's task was much broader. He was called to be a messenger of God not only to Judah but also to the nations, and not only simply for doom but also for hope. Jeremiah was to be one of the two "transition" prophets (the other was Ezekiel) who, because of the peculiar historical circumstances of their time, were also privileged to speak words of hope in addition to the words of doom. Jeremiah's task was

> ". . . to pluck up and to break down,
> to destroy and to overthrow,
> to build and to plant."
>   —Jeremiah 1:10

It is interesting to note that there is no record here of Jeremiah's ever having said "Yes" to this election. That he had to have accepted it is obvious, but it is a curious fact that throughout his life he always felt that he had had no choice in the matter, that Yahweh had "rigged" the game against him (see 20:7-9)!

Connected with this call account of Jeremiah are two "visions," the meanings of which in a real sense summarize the entire ministry and message of this great prophet. The first is a short account of what Jeremiah learned from observing a rod from an almond tree.

> And the word of the LORD came to me, saying, "Jeremiah, what do you see?" And I said, "I see a rod of almond." Then the LORD said to me, "You have seen well, for I am watching over my word to perform it" (1:11-12).

Visions were one of the more usual means by which holy people received messages from God in those days. Again the prophets are no exceptions. A vision to the prophet in that time, however, did not always mean something seen in a state of ecstatic trance. A vision could also be a message from God which came to someone by meditating on some simple, everyday item. For example, Amos was meditating on a plumb line and understood from it something of God's truth (see Amos 7:7ff.).

The Semitic peoples were also very adept at "word play," something that is often called a pun in our time. The Semitic languages lend themselves to such activity because the language is written in consonants only, the vowels being added by the reader. One can readily see how such a device would fit very well into the prophetic "vision" motif. Another example from Amos will help to understand this phenomenon. Amos is asked by Yahweh what he sees (Amos 8:1-2). He replies, "A basket of summer fruit." In Hebrew the word for "summer fruit" is *qyts,* (pronounced *kâ yits*). But whereas Amos saw a basket of summer fruit, he learned that there was in that simple, ordinary item a message from Yahweh for the people. For the consonants *qyts* can also be the word for the "end" (pronounced *kêts)*. In this "vision" Amos understood that Yahweh was telling him something about the land and Yahweh's plans for it. What do you see, Amos? A basket of summer fruit. No, Amos. What you see is that the end is coming upon the people!

All that is by way of introducing these verses in Jeremiah where he "sees" something ordinary, a stick from the almond tree. The Hebrew for this is *shqd,* pronounced *shakêd.* But Jeremiah learned that there was a message from Yahweh in this "vision," for the letters *shqd* can also mean to "watch," *shôkêd.* From this Jeremiah learned that Yahweh was "watching" over his word to see that it came to pass.

The reason for this passage being placed here in the Book of Jeremiah is probably to set the stage for much of Jeremiah's teaching and life. Yahweh had promised Jeremiah that the words he uttered for Yahweh would definitely come to pass, something that Jeremiah often forgot through the course of his tortured ministry. He said that Yahweh would destroy the nation, but the people pointed to the temple and said that they were safe. Jeremiah said that he had become a "laughing-stock" among the people. He was always reminded, however, that Yahweh was "watching" over his word to bring it to fulfillment. The meaning of the vision then is one that Jeremiah needed throughout his life. The teaching is quite appropriately placed here at the beginning of Jeremiah's ministry.

The word of the LORD came to me a second time, saying, "What do you see?" And I said, "I see a boiling pot, facing away from the north." Then the LORD said to me, "Out of the north evil shall break forth upon all the inhabitants of the land. For, lo, I am calling all the tribes of the kingdoms of the north, says the LORD; and they shall come and every one shall set his throne at the entrance of the gates of Jerusalem, against all its walls round about, and against all the cities of Judah. And I will utter my judgments against them, for all their wickedness in forsaking me; they have burned incense to other gods, and worshiped the works of their own hands. But you, gird up your loins; arise, and say to them everything that I command you. Do not be dismayed by them, lest I dismay you before them. And I, behold, I make you this day a fortified city, an iron pillar, and bronze walls, against the whole land, against the kings of Judah, its princes, its priests, and the people of the land. They will fight against you; but they shall not prevail against you, for I am with you, says the LORD, to deliver you" (1:13-19).

The second vision which has been placed within the context of Jeremiah's call revolves around a boiling pot which faces away from the north, probably meaning that the contents are being poured out. This passage does not contain a play on words, but Jeremiah learned something while watching a boiling pot which was tipped from north toward the south and whose contents came pouring out.

The prophets of Israel and Judah almost always depicted and understood Yahweh's judgment on their nations in terms of military conquest. After all, war is one of the worst punishments that can be inflicted upon any people. They understood that when God judged his people, it would be by means of a military defeat. And most of the prophets speculated about which country would be used to execute God's will.

No less was this true with Jeremiah. From observing the boiling pot tipped over from the north, he came to the conclusion that the enemy would come from the north. This understanding was not all that marvelous, however. As one knows if familiar with the geography of that part of the world, there were only two ways an enemy could come into the land of Palestine: from the north or from the south. To the west lay the ocean and to the east lay a large desert. Therefore any invader had to come from the south or southwest (Egypt) or from the north. Any nation that lay north or east of Judah would have had to enter the area through the valley of Jezreel (or the Plain of Esdraelon) toward the northern part of the country. Jeremiah did not think that Egypt would be the instrument of God's judgment. Therefore, whoever would be used as that instrument would come from that northerly direction. There are numerous passages that refer to this "foe from the north" (see 4:5-8, 11-13, 15-17; 5:10-17; 6:1-8; 8:16-17).

The question that scholars debate revolves around exactly what nation Jeremiah had in mind as the "foe from the north." Earlier scholarship identified these invaders as a roving barbaric people known as the Scythians who were thought to have been in that area of the world about 625 B.C. But further investigation has raised some questions about the existence of the Scythians and/or their presence in Palestine. Coupled with this is the question of the time when

Jeremiah began his public ministry. If he began at the later date, as many are now arguing (and is the position taken here), the Scythians, even if they had been on the scene in 626, were by 609 entirely gone. It seems best, therefore, to understand the enemy from the north as Babylonia. Jeremiah, throughout most of the recorded data included in the book bearing his name, seems to have Babylonia specifically in mind. Whether he knew this from the very beginning of his ministry or gradually came to know it in the course of the events happening to the world and to Judah cannot be stated without equivocation. But he did know that the enemy was to come from the north and (sooner or later) that it would be Babylonia.

This was a significant part of Jeremiah's teaching. He specifically told the people and the political leaders that it was the will of Yahweh to submit to the yoke of the Babylonians. For this he was almost killed on numerous occasions. This also is anticipated in these verses. Jeremiah was told that he would be forced to stand against all the powers, people, and pressures of the land. They would fight against him. But Jeremiah was told and given assurance at the beginning of his lonely ministry that they would not "prevail against [him]." For Yahweh would be there to stand by him.

Questions for Further Study

1. Discuss the importance of the biblical idea of election. Can you think of other examples where people were called to perform a specific task for God?

2. Do you think people are still called today for similar purposes?

3. How do the two "visions" (1:11-12, 13-19) serve as a foundation for Jeremiah's long and lonely ministry?

3

Jeremiah's Resistance to His Call

There are included among the oracles of Jeremiah several passages in which Jeremiah argues with God and tries to abandon his call. These passages are usually called the "confessions" of Jeremiah. Whether they were ever uttered publicly is not known, but in all probability they were not. These passages are found in the following portions of the book: 11:18–12:6; 15:10-21; 17:12(14)-18; 18:18-23; 20:7-18. One notes that these all occur between chapters 11 and 21 and may at one time have been collected together by themselves.

> The LORD made it known to me and I knew;
>   then thou didst show me their evil deeds.
> But I was like a gentle lamb
>   led to the slaughter.
> I did not know it was against me
>   they devised schemes, saying,
> "Let us destroy the tree with its fruit,
>   let us cut him off from the land of the living,
>   that his name be remembered no more."
> But, O LORD of hosts, who judgest righteously,
>   who triest the heart and the mind,
> let me see thy vengeance upon them,
>   for to thee have I committed my cause.

Therefore thus says the LORD concerning the men of Anathoth, who seek your life, and say, "Do not prophesy in the

name of the LORD, or you will die by our hand"—therefore thus
says the LORD of hosts: "Behold, I will punish them; the young men
shall die by the sword; their sons and their daughters shall die by
famine; and none of them shall be left. For I will bring evil upon the
men of Anathoth, the year of their punishment."

> Righteous art thou, O LORD,
>   when I complain to thee;
> yet I would plead my case before thee.
> Why does the way of the wicked prosper?
>   Why do all who are treacherous thrive?
> Thou plantest them, and they take root;
>   they grow and bring forth fruit;
> thou art near in their mouth
>   and far from their heart.
> But thou, O LORD, knowest me;
>   thou seest me, and triest my mind toward thee.
> Pull them out like sheep for the slaughter,
> and set them apart for the day of slaughter.
> How long will the land mourn,
>   and the grass of every field wither?
> For the wickedness of those who dwell in it
>   the beasts and the birds are swept away,
>   because men said, "He will not see our latter end."
> "If you have raced with men on foot,
>   and they have wearied you,
>   how will you compete with horses?
> And if in a safe land you fall down,
>   how will you do in the jungle of the Jordan?
> For even your brothers and the house of your father,
>   even they have dealt treacherously with you;
>   they are in full cry after you;
> believe them not,
>   though they speak fair words to you."
>   —Jeremiah 11:18–12:6

The question arises when considering this passage as to whether
11:18-20 and 12:1-6 may be separate poems or whether they should be
considered as a single unity. The answer to that question, however,
does not really affect the interpretation of the material; therefore we

shall not spend our time in an attempt to unravel that mystery. The first part of the passage (11:18-20) finds Jeremiah complaining to God, because he had just discovered a plot against his life. He had heard whisperings about such a plot but did not realize at the time that the proceedings were to be directed at him. Exactly why this plot was devised or when cannot be determined from the text. From verses 21-23 it appears that the ones who instigated this evil business were the people of his own city, Anathoth. Could it be that his own kinsmen were involved as well?

Jeremiah did not take such activity against him lightly, however. He asked Yahweh to allow him to see those who sought to kill him punished. It is a totally human reaction, but it certainly does not qualify for the "forgiveness-of-the-year" award!

The second part of this confession is found in 12:1-6. At this point Jeremiah was wrestling with some of the ambiguities of the world. At the time of Jeremiah there was in effect the religious idea that the good are rewarded and the evil are punished. In those times the reward and/or punishment had to come during one's lifetime, because there was no thought about an afterlife with rewards and/or punishments. Their idea was that when people died, they went to a place called *Sheol*. It was the abode of the dead where all—rich and poor, free and slave, male and female, good and bad—went upon death. It was a place of gloom and darkness where the "personalities" of people resided after physical death. It was the weakest kind of life one could imagine, but the person was still conscious and aware of what was going on.

Naturally with such an idea as this, it came to be the accepted premise that good and evil were rewarded *in this life*. There was no other place for this to occur. In addition to this kind of thinking, another idea was also exceedingly important to the people of that era. Since Sheol was so gloomy, it came to be held that in some way (not ever clearly defined) the gloom of Sheol could be made less burdensome if one still had a connection with the land of the living. This connection was understood to be one's physical offspring, one's children.

The importance of that thought can be clearly seen in the old law that was continued perhaps even into the time of Jesus (see Mark 12:18ff.). This was the *levirate* law (see Deuteronomy 25:5-10). The idea involved in this requirement was that there should be a child raised up for a deceased husband if he died childless. It was the *duty* of the next of kin (usually a brother of the deceased) to take the widow, have sexual relations with her, and raise up a child which would then be considered as the child of the deceased. This would insure him a connection with the land of the living. One must not think of this law as a license for sexual promiscuity; far from it—this was considered to be a very serious obligation which must be carried out (see the story of Judah and Tamar in Genesis 38). One can already see something of the sacrifice Jeremiah was called upon to make, because Yahweh, as a sign to the people, forbade Jeremiah to marry (see Jeremiah 16:1ff.).

To return to the passage under consideration, however, it appeared to Jeremiah that the good were not being rewarded and the evil were not being punished. And he wanted to know why! He saw the good people exploited by the wicked and unscrupulous. He saw the nation in a state of moral decay because of these evil people. If indeed the orthodox theology of the time were correct, these people who were wicked should have been in the process of receiving their just deserts. But alas, they were not, and even nature suffered because of their sin (see 12:4a,b). Jeremiah, not only because of the threats against his own life but also because of his sensitive nature, asked why this was allowed to happen.

As is usually the case in such situations of questioning the ways of the world, Jeremiah did not receive any answer to his question. In fact, he was told that he "ain't seen nuthin' yet!"

> "If you have raced with men on foot,
>   and they have wearied you,
> how will you compete with horses?
> And if in a safe land you fall,
>   how will you do in the jungle of the Jordan?"
> —Jeremiah 12:5

Another possible translation of the latter part of this verse which demonstrates the essential message would be something like, "If while wading in a shallow pond you slip and fall, what will you do when the tidal wave comes crashing down upon you?"

In other words, things would get worse before they got better. There is in biblical teachings the distinct idea that evil must be allowed to run its course. This is especially true in the literature known as apocalyptic (see Daniel and Revelation), but the concept is also found in other places. This is the idea that is relayed to Jeremiah.

While that kind of message is not one to encourage hope by itself, the biblical writers were all of one accord that God, being the type of God they understood him to be, can and will stand by his own even in the midst of unspeakable evil. He does not promise his people—not even those who are most special, such as Jeremiah—an escape from the hardships of the world. Rather, the promise is that they will never be *totally* overcome by evil and that God will be with them in the midst of the trouble.

Jeremiah was told essentially this. He was encouraged to remember that even in his call he had been warned that the going would be rough (see 1:16-19). He was promised, however, that the enemies of his work would not prevail over him. In addition to this he was given a bit of very practical and realistic advice: Do not trust people whom you suspect of plotting against you even if they "speak fair words to you" (12:6). Even with God on one's side, human reason and caution must be exercised!

Woe is me, my mother, that you bore me, a man of strife and contention to the whole land! I have not lent, nor have I borrowed, yet all of them curse me. So let it be, O LORD, if I have not entreated thee for their good, if I have not pleaded with thee on behalf of the enemy in the time of trouble and in the time of distress! Can one break iron, iron from the north, and bronze?

"Your wealth and your treasures I will give as spoil, without price, for all your sins, throughout all your territory. I will make you serve your enemies in a land which you do not know, for in my anger a fire is kindled which shall burn for ever."

O LORD, thou knowest;
   remember me and visit me,
   and take vengeance for me on my persecutors.
In thy forbearance take me not away;
   know that for thy sake I bear reproach.
Thy words were found, and I ate them,
   and thy words became to me a joy
   and the delight of my heart;
for I am called by thy name,
   O LORD, God of hosts.
I did not sit in the company of merrymakers,
   nor did I rejoice;

I sat alone, because thy hand was upon me,
for thou hadst filled me with indignation.
Why is my pain unceasing,
my wound incurable,
refusing to be healed?
Wilt thou be to me like a deceitful brook,
like waters that fail?

Therefore thus says the LORD:
"If you return, I will restore you,
and you shall stand before me.
If you utter what is precious, and not what is worthless,
you shall be as my mouth.
They shall turn to you,
but you shall not turn to them.
And I will make you to this people
a fortified wall of bronze;
they will fight against you,
but they shall not prevail over you,
for I am with you
to save you and deliver you,
says the LORD.
I will deliver you out of the hand of the wicked,
and redeem you from the grasp of the ruthless."
—Jeremiah 15:10-21

These verses again demonstrate Jeremiah's feeling of loneliness and, to be honest, doubt. He rued his birth and agonized over his lot in life. Obviously he was a person who liked to be around people and to share in the fellowship of their merriment. His calling, however, caused him to have to live his life basically alone (15:17).

The sense of the passage seems to be also that his preaching of the word of Yahweh was an embarrassment to him. The message of doom had not yet come to pass; he was the object of ridicule and abuse because the land was still intact. Things had not really changed all that much. Jeremiah, like almost every human being, wanted to see some kind of external sign which would at least give him some confidence that what he believed and was saying was, in fact, correct. This kind of thinking seems to lie behind the saying of verse 18.

At this point he called Yahweh a "deceitful brook," "waters that fail." The figure is an appropriate one for that area of the world. There are the numerous streambeds (called wadis) which flow with water during the rainy season of the year. But when the summer and its heat begin to dry up the land, these wadis also become dry. The picture here is that of Jeremiah saying to God, "When I don't really need you, you are there. But when the times become difficult, I can't find you anywhere. You are a fraud!"

Jeremiah was then told in stern language that if he repented and spoke the truth, God would be with him to deliver him from evil people. He would be a "fortified wall of bronze," standing strong, defending what was behind it from evil. God told him specifically that he would not be rescued from hardship; "they will fight against you" (15:20). In a sense Jeremiah had to renew his commitment to his calling.

The lesson which he learned from this seems to be that commitment to God and to truth and to justice and to right cannot rest on external manifestations of success and accomplishment. Real religious faith has to transcend that kind of thinking. The question that can be raised here is whether someone who has been called by God (elected, no less) could reject that election and cease to be a servant. Even though the text does not explicitly state that position, it seems to be clear that the choice was left to Jeremiah. In other words, Jeremiah could have rejected his election and ceased to be a spokesman for God.

He was challenged to repent, and in the biblical texts repentance is left to the choice of the person or groups involved. Jeremiah had to renew his commitment to God and his work. God's promise was the same: even though he would not be protected from hardships and tragedies, Jeremiah would stand through them all by the strength of God.

> Heal me, O Lord, and I shall be healed;
>   save me, and I shall be saved;
>   for thou art my praise.
> Behold, they say to me,
>   "Where is the word of the Lord?
>   Let it come!"
> I have not pressed thee to send evil,
>   nor have I desired the day of disaster,
>   thou knowest;

> that which came out of my lips
> was before thy face.
> Be not a terror to me;
> thou art my refuge in the day of evil.
> Let those be put to shame who persecute me,
> but let me not be put to shame;
> let them be dismayed,
> but let me not be dismayed;
> bring upon them the day of evil;
> destroy them with double destruction!
> —Jeremiah 17:14-18

This "confession" of Jeremiah is quite similar to the others already examined. Jeremiah had proclaimed the word of Yahweh; it had been a word of destruction and doom, but it had not as yet come to pass. Because of this his countrymen were angered; to their minds Jeremiah was a traitor, a malicious and vengeful person who was attempting to destroy his own people out of spite.

There is contained in this passage, however, an insight into the soul of the prophetic messenger which is too often overlooked in the study of the prophetic movement. There are many interpreters of the prophets who are turned off by their constant condemnation of the people and their predictions of coming disaster. These people feel that the prophets were weird or perverted personalities who obtained some psychological satisfaction in these proclamations against their own people.

But that is to miss the point of the prophetic ministry. These prophets were called by God to deliver his message. They were not at all happy with the message they were given to proclaim. In contrast to receiving some psychological glee from this activity, most of them would have preferred to remain silent. They loved their lands and their nations. It grieved them to see the intensity of evil building to a fever pitch from which there could be no repentance and therefore no deliverance. Amos, for example, was one of the most devastating of all the prophets in his proclamation of doom; yet Amos interceded for the people before Yahweh. He tried to persuade God to change his mind, to put aside the judgment (see Amos 7).

So too with Jeremiah—he loved his land and even those wicked people in the land. He hoped for their repentance, but it never came. He sadly realized that they were so far immersed in their sins that they could not distinguish between good and evil and were in fact incapable of doing good (see chapters 2–6 especially).

As we see in this passage, Jeremiah told God that it was not his idea to preach a "day of disaster." He told God that he had only spoken what God required to be said. Since he had done that, however, he wished for some vindication of his message. This may have been, however, because he felt that if some disaster came, perhaps the people would believe him and repent. Perhaps there would yet be time. It was a hope against hope, however. And Jeremiah still wished for vindication against his enemies, an extremely human response: ". . . destroy them with double destruction!"

Then they said, "Come, let us make plots against Jeremiah, for the law shall not perish from the priest, nor counsel from the wise, nor the word from the prophet. Come, let us smite him with the tongue, and let us not heed any of his words."
Give heed to me, O LORD,
    and hearken to my plea.
Is evil a recompense for good?
    Yet they have dug a pit for my life.
Remember how I stood before thee
    to speak good for them,
    to turn away thy wrath from them.
Therefore deliver up their children to famine;
    give them over to the power of the sword,
let their wives become childless and widowed.
May their men meet death by pestilence,
    their youths be slain by the sword in battle.
May a cry be heard from their houses,
    when thou bringest the marauder suddenly upon them!
For they have dug a pit to take me,
    and laid snares for my feet.
Yet, thou, O LORD, knowest
    all their plotting to slay me.
Forgive not their iniquity,
    nor blot out their sin from thy sight.
Let them be overthrown before thee;
    deal with them in the time of thine anger.
                   —Jeremiah 18:18-23

The setting for this particular "confession" of Jeremiah is found in another plot or attempt on his life, this time by the religious leaders. They obviously had had more than enough of his teaching directed toward them (see for example 2:8; 8:8; 9:23f.; etc. We shall study Jeremiah's relationship with and teachings directed toward these groups shortly). At this point they turned and were allied against Jeremiah.

What they planned to do was to speak evil against him (and we recall that this is more than a recitation of mere empty words). And further they planned to ignore his words. This may refer to Jeremiah's preaching per se or it may refer to anything Jeremiah could say in his defense. It is interesting to note that the Greek translation of this passage reads, "Let us heed all his words." If this is the original reading, the implication is that they were going to listen carefully to everything Jeremiah said, probably in the hope of entrapping him in some legal technicality or "slip of the tongue." In either case the meaning is clear. They planned to do away with Jeremiah if they possibly could.

What follows then is Jeremiah's most vicious attack on his tormentors. The reference in verse 20 to a "pit" may reflect the later time when Jeremiah had been cast into an empty cistern to die. If that is the background of the passage, it is much easier to understand the bitterness and even viciousness of his outburst. He had been thrown into a dark, slimy hole with no light, which was probably infested with rats and insects and worms, and left to starve to death (see chapter 38:1-13). The intensity of his feelings here can certainly be understood, if not condoned. There are some interpreters who simply deny that Jeremiah uttered these words, believing that these thoughts are beneath that of a true servant of God. There is no reason, however, to deny these words to Jeremiah. God's servants remain all too human in spite of their election! What Jeremiah had endured at the hands of these people, however, was unthinkable. Bitterness is not a virtue and should not be condoned, but we can certainly understand Jeremiah's feeling.

> O LORD, thou hast deceived me,
>   and I was deceived;
> thou art stronger than I,
>   and thou hast prevailed.
> I have become a laughingstock all the day;

every one mocks me.
For whenever I speak, I cry out,
    I shout, "Violence and destruction!"
For the word of the LORD has become for me
    a reproach and derision all day long.
If I say, "I will not mention him,
    or speak any more in his name,"
there is in my heart as it were a burning fire
    shut up in my bones,
and I am weary with holding it in,
    and I cannot.
For I hear many whispering.
    Terror is on every side!
"Denounce him! Let us denounce him!"
    say all my familiar friends,
    watching for my fall.
"Perhaps he will be deceived,
    then we can overcome him,
    and take our revenge on him."
But the LORD is with me as a dread warrior;
    therefore my persecutors will stumble,
    they will not overcome me.
They will be greatly shamed,
    for they will not succeed.
Their eternal dishonor
    will never be forgotten.
O LORD of hosts, who triest the righteous,
    who seest the heart and the mind,
let me see thy vengeance upon them,
    for to thee have I committed my cause.
Sing to the LORD;
    praise the LORD!
For he has delivered the life of the needy
    from the hand of evildoers.
Cursed be the day
    on which I was born!
The day when my mother bore me,
    let it not be blessed!
Cursed be the man
    who brought the news to my father,

> "A son is born to you,"
>   making him very glad.
> Let that man be like the cities
>   which the LORD overthrew without pity;
> let him hear a cry in the morning
>   and an alarm at noon,
> because he did not kill me in the womb;
>   so my mother would have been my grave,
>   and her womb for ever great.
> Why did I come forth from the womb
>   to see toil and sorrow,
>   and spend my days in shame?
>   —Jeremiah 20:7-18

This last "confession" (whether it was in reality the last, we do not know) is placed within the context of the Book of Jeremiah in a setting in which Jeremiah had just suffered an ignominious humiliation. His message, which he delivered to the elders of the people (see chapter 19), enraged the chief priest, Pashhur, who had Jeremiah beaten and publicly displayed in "stocks." We do not know exactly in what precise form the "stocks" were made, but from our own history we know that they were very uncomfortable and dehumanizing. To have been beaten, locked into those inhuman devices, and left in that position for a day and a night would have surely placed Jeremiah in a state of mind where a complaint to God would have been in order!

As he began this lament, Jeremiah said that he had become a "laughing-stock all the day." It may be that this was intended as a pun in the Hebrew text. In this passage the prophet said that Yahweh had "seduced" him. He had suffered humiliation and ridicule and abuse for speaking the word of God. He had warned the people of the impending disaster, but so far the disaster had not come. Because of that the ridicule heaped upon Jeremiah had become even more abusive.

Jeremiah decided that the solution to that situation was simply to refrain from speaking the message Yahweh had given him to preach. But even then he felt helpless, for he could not keep the message locked up within himself. It became like a "burning fire shut up in my bones" (20:9) which could not be controlled. When a sensitive person such as Jeremiah knows the truth and is committed to the truth and knows that the truth can help his people, it is impossible to remain silent.

Jeremiah continued to hear the murmurings of the people about him. They waited for him to make a mistake so that they could heap additional abuse upon him. In this confession, however, Jeremiah seemed to have learned that Yahweh was indeed with him. He believed that his "persecutors will stumble." In this passage also Jeremiah did not seem to be so intent upon their destruction as he had been on some previous occasions (see 15:1ff.; 17:18; 18:21ff.). Here he simply knew that he was right and that Yahweh would vindicate him and show that they had been wrong. What he asked was that he be allowed to see the judgment upon them when it came.

The last section of this passage (verses 14-18) may be from another time in Jeremiah's life. The mood and tone shifts from a kind of quiet strength to a moment of almost total despair. He lamented the day of his birth (compare Job 3:3ff.) and thought that it would have been best for him to have died at or before birth. His life had been hard and lonely, and bitterness had become his constant companion. It is a credit to the integrity of his person that in spite of all these problems and fears, he stood firm to the end of his life proclaiming the word of God as he knew it.

Questions for Further Discussion

1. How is it possible for a servant of God to have the kinds of feelings that Jeremiah did toward God? Toward his people?

2. In all of these tribulations Jeremiah never contemplated suicide. Why do you think he did not?

3. What did Jeremiah learn from his sufferings? About God? About himself? About people?

4
Jeremiah's Relationship with the Political Leaders

During the course of his ministry, Jeremiah encountered considerable opposition from those in positions of authority in Judah. These included both the religious as well as the political leaders, and a considerable amount of his teaching is directly related to his ongoing struggle with them. We shall examine his relationship with these groups and the teachings he directed toward them.

First of all, Jeremiah had an almost constant struggle with the political authorities, especially the kings. It is clear that these leaders respected the prophet even though they may not have agreed with what he said. In fact, they seemed at times even to fear him!

There is very little which is said about King Josiah even though according to tradition Jeremiah is supposed to have prophesied during seventeen years of Josiah's reign. It is very clear that Jeremiah respected and admired this man, what he was and what he was trying to do for the nation. In 22:15 Jeremiah gives him a stirring vote of confidence (but it is a backward look after his death):

> "Did not your [Jehoiakim's] father eat and drink
> and do justice and righteousness?
> Then it was well with him.
> He judged the cause of the poor and needy;
> then it was well.
> Is not this to know me?"
> says the LORD.
> —Jeremiah 22:15b-16

57

Josiah's untimely and wasteful death (caused by his own lack of insight and realism) opened the doors for the last days of Judah.

As already noted earlier, after Josiah's death the king of Egypt placed Jehoiakim on the throne of Judah. Because of that, Jehoiakim's loyalties always lay with Egypt; and even though Judah became a vassal of Babylonia, Jehoiakim sought every opportunity to rebel against her. He was a selfish ruler who cared little for the people. This is seen clearly in the fact that soon after he came to the throne, he decided to build a new palace. The splendor of the place and therefore its cost were far beyond what the people of the land could afford. And to top it off, Jehoiakim used forced labor for the building of the project. Jeremiah's oracle in 22:13-17 speaks precisely to the occasion.

> "Woe to him who builds his house by unrighteousness,
>   and his upper rooms by injustice;
> who makes his neighbor serve him for nothing,
>   and does not give him his wages;
> who says, 'I will build myself a great house
>   with spacious upper rooms,'
> and cuts out windows for it,
>   paneling it with cedar,
>   and painting it with vermilion.
> Do you think you are a king
>   because you compete in cedar?
> Did not your father eat and drink
>   and do justice and righteousness?
>   Then it was well with him.
> He judged the cause of the poor and needy;
>   then it was well.
> Is not this to know me?
>   says the LORD.
> But you have eyes and heart
>   only for your dishonest gain,
> for shedding innocent blood,
>   and for practicing oppression and violence."
>   —Jeremiah 22:13-17

Attached to this oracle about Jehoiakim is another in which Jeremiah utters a scathing denunciation of the ruler.

Therefore thus says the LORD concerning Jehoiakim the son of
Josiah, king of Judah:
"They shall not lament for him, saying,
'Ah my brother!' or 'Ah sister!'
They shall not lament for him, saying,
'Ah lord!' or 'Ah his majesty!'
With the burial of an ass he shall be buried,
dragged and cast forth beyond the gates of Jerusalem."
                                                              —Jeremiah 22:18-19

It is little wonder that Jehoiakim hated Jeremiah! This prediction of
Jeremiah did not come to pass, however, for Jehoiakim died shortly
before Nebuchadnezzar took Jerusalem the first time (598 B.C.).

Not only did the king hate and pursue Jeremiah, but also he
obviously tolerated no prophet or priest who failed to accede to his
wishes and speak kindly to and for him. In 26:20-23 we read that he
sent a group of people to Egypt to return a prophet who had spoken
harshly about him. The text says: "and they fetched Uriah from Egypt
and brought him to King Jehoiakim, who slew him with the sword
and cast his dead body into the burial place of the common people"
(26:23). Not only did Jehoiakim refuse a proper trial under the law,
but also he executed the poor fellow on the spot and refused to allow
him a proper burial, a great disgrace in that time. Given the
circumstances it is a marvel that Jeremiah was not killed!

So bitter was Jehoiakim's hatred of Jeremiah that we are told
that Jeremiah on several occasions had to remain in hiding (see 36:5,
19, 26). During one of these occasions Yahweh commanded Jeremiah
to dictate the words of his oracles so that they might be read to the
king and to the people (36:1ff.). After this was done, Baruch took the
scroll and read it in the temple. The princes of the land heard of the
message and had it read to them. Whereupon they took it to
Jehoiakim so that he could also hear the words of warning for the
nation.

As the scroll was read to the king, he took a knife and bit by bit
tossed the scroll into the fire which was burning in the room. The
action is characteristic of the king's utter disdain for the word of God
or the sanctity of God's messengers or the people of the land. For at
this point in history Jeremiah, even though he knew that Yahweh was
going to give the land over to the Babylonians, also saw that if the
king would not lead a revolt against Babylon, the land and the people

could be spared excessive suffering and destruction. But Jehoiakim could not be reached, not even by the word of God. The judgment would be certain. "'I will punish him and his offspring and his servants for their iniquity; I will bring upon them, and upon the inhabitants of Jerusalem, and upon the men of Judah, all the evil that I have pronounced against them, but they would not hear'" (36:31).

We have already noted that Jehoiakim died before Nebuchadnezzar was able to capture Jerusalem for the first time (598/7). His death remains something of a mystery, and, even though there is no direct evidence for it, some have conjectured that assassination might have been the cause. (If true, this saved him some suffering at the hands of the Babylonians, which may have been more than he deserved!) Whatever did happen, he had departed and his son, Jehoiachin (sometimes called Coniah), ruled for a few months until the city fell to the Babylonians. He was carried off to exile in Babylonia. For him Jeremiah had some sincere compassion.

The basic word of Jeremiah for Jehoiachin was nevertheless negative, i.e., that he would not return from exile and would not rule over Judah again. This message had to be constantly repeated, for some other prophets were saying that he would return and rule again in the land (see 28:1-4). The basic text which depicts Jeremiah's teaching about Jehoiachin is 22:24-30.

"As I live, says the LORD, though Coniah the son of Jehoiakim, king of Judah, were the signet ring on my right hand, yet I would tear you off and give you into the hand of those who seek your life, into the hand of those of whom you are afraid, even into the hand of Nebuchadrezzar king of Babylon and into the hand of the Chaldeans. I will hurl you and the mother who bore you into another country, where you were not born, and there you shall die. But to the land to which they will long to return, there they shall not return."
Is this man Coniah a despised, broken pot,
a vessel no one cares for?
Why are he and his children hurled and cast
into a land which they do not know?
O land, land, land,
hear the word of the LORD!
Thus says the LORD:
"Write this man down as childless,

a man who shall not succeed in his days;
for none of his offspring shall succeed
in sitting on the throne of David,
and ruling again in Judah."
—Jeremiah 22:24-30

Jeremiah was correct; Jehoiachin and his family longed to return but did not return. And none of his sons ever sat upon the throne of Judah.

After the fall of the city and the land to the forces of Nebuchadnezzar in 598–597, Jehoiachin and his family were carried into exile. Zedekiah (whose name was Mattaniah) was placed on the throne. He was evidently a son of Jehoiakim and therefore of the royal line. This gesture was surely made by the Babylonians to attempt to show as much leniency toward the country as possible. Zedekiah, however, was a man of "good intentions" but without moral strength to carry out what he knew to be right. He was constantly torn between his pro-Egyptian advisers and the words of the great prophet. His relationship with Jeremiah is an interesting account.

Several incidents involving Jeremiah with Zedekiah occurred. Most of these revolved around Zedekiah's desire to know the word of Yahweh from Jeremiah. But what he hoped for was a positive affirmation that God was going to perform a gigantic miracle and deliver the land from its enemies.

At the very beginning of Zedekiah's reign Jeremiah attempted to demonstrate to him and to the people that it was the will of Yahweh to submit to the Babylonians. If they would be submissive, things could even now go well for them. To illustrate the point, he made a yoke (similar to that placed on oxen) and wore it about the streets of the city.[1] He wanted to make it clear that Yahweh would punish any nation (27:8) which did not submit to Babylonia. The specific charge is directed both to the people and to the rulers, especially to Zedekiah.

But other voices were being raised. Another prophet, Hananiah, proclaimed in the name of Yahweh that Babylon would be destroyed, that Jehoiachin and all the exiles would be returning home within two

---

[1] This type of behavior seems quite "unusual" to us, but it belongs to a type of action known as "prophetic signs." There are several of these types of incidents related to Jeremiah's ministry which will be discussed more fully later. See chapter 6 of this book.

years (see 28:1-4). He even took the yoke bars of Jeremiah and broke them, supposedly demonstrating and effecting the demise of Babylon's power (28:10-11). Jeremiah went away to meditate on those events, whereupon the word of the Lord came to him again. He was told this time to take iron bars! (Unless Hananiah were Clark Kent in disguise, there was no way he could break this new yoke!) Jeremiah did as he was commanded. He chastised Hananiah for encouraging the people to believe in a lie! Hananiah was told that within a year he would die—and he did (see 28:12-17).

On another occasion Zedekiah sent word to Jeremiah as follows: "Inquire of the LORD for us, for Nebuchadnezzar king of Babylon is making war against us; perhaps the LORD will deal with us according to all his wonderful deeds, and will make him withdraw from us" (21:2). It is not known exactly when this inquiry was made, but it must have come shortly before the second siege of the city in 587-586. This was caused by Zedekiah's rebellion against Babylonia which was encouraged by Egypt and his pro-Egyptian counselors.

The answer of Jeremiah was not exactly what Zedekiah had in mind. The prophet encouraged submission to Babylonia as he had done all along. While this message was not what the king or the people wished to hear, Jeremiah felt that this was the will of Yahweh both in terms of his judgment on the land for its evil and in terms of his grace for the land in alleviating excessive suffering and hardship. In this particular response to Zedekiah's question, probably to emphasize his point, he even encouraged people to desert the city so that they could be delivered from the horrors of the siege and its aftermath. This kind of advice did not win Jeremiah any friends at the court. The full reply to Zedekiah is worth noting.

> Then Jeremiah said to them: "Thus you shall say to Zedekiah, 'Thus says the LORD, the God of Israel: Behold, I will turn back the weapons of war which are in your hands and with which you are fighting against the king of Babylon and against the Chaldeans who are besieging you outside the walls; and I will bring them together into the midst of this city. I myself will fight against you with outstretched hand and strong arm, in anger, and in fury, and in great wrath. And I will smite the inhabitants of this city, both man and beast; they shall die of a great pestilence. Afterward, says the LORD, I will give Zedekiah king of Judah, and his servants, and the people in this city who survive the pestilence, sword, and

famine, into the hand of Nebuchadrezzar king of Babylon and into the hand of their enemies, into the hand of those who seek their lives. He shall smite them with the edge of the sword; he shall not pity them, or spare them, or have compassion.'

"And to this people you shall say: 'Thus says the LORD: Behold, I set before you the way of life and the way of death. He who stays in this city shall die by the sword, by famine, and by pestilence; but he who goes out and surrenders to the Chaldeans who are besieging you shall live and shall have his life as a prize of war. For I have set my face against this city for evil and not for good, says the LORD: it shall be given into the hand of the king of Babylon, and he shall burn it with fire'" (21:3-10).

Another incident that reflects the kind of leader Zedekiah was can be seen in the account of 34:8-22. This particular event took place while the city was under siege in 587-586. In order to relieve themselves of any responsibilities for giving food to their slaves, Zedekiah and the rulers decreed that all the slaves were hereby free! This took place as city after city in the land had fallen to the Babylonians, and Jerusalem, it appeared, would be next.

At that moment, however, an Egyptian force had begun to move into Palestine from the southwest. To counter that threat, the siege against Jerusalem was momentarily lifted (see 34:21f.; 37:5). When that happened, Zedekiah and the rulers rescinded the order freeing the slaves! This brought a scathing response from Jeremiah.

The word of the LORD came to Jeremiah from the LORD: "Thus says the LORD, the God of Israel: I made a covenant with your fathers when I brought them out of the land of Egypt, out of the house of bondage, saying, 'At the end of six years each of you must set free the fellow Hebrew who has been sold to you and has served you six years; you must set him free from your service.' But your fathers did not listen to me or incline their ears to me. You recently repented and did what was right in my eyes by proclaiming liberty, each to his neighbor, and you made a covenant before me in the house which is called by my name; but then you turned around and profaned my name when each of you took back his male and female slaves, whom you had set free according to their desire, and you brought them into subjection to be your slaves. Therefore, thus says the LORD: You have not obeyed me by proclaiming liberty,

every one to his brother and to his neighbor; behold, I proclaim to
you liberty to the sword, to pestilence, and to famine, says the
LORD. I will make you a horror to all the kingdoms of the earth.
And the men who transgressed my covenant and did not keep the
terms of the covenant which they made before me, I will make like
the calf which they cut in two and passed between its parts—the
princes of Judah, the princes of Jerusalem, the eunuchs, the priests,
and all the people of the land who passed between the parts of the
calf; and I will give them into the hand of their enemies and into the
hand of those who seek their lives. Their dead bodies shall be food
for the birds of the air and the beasts of the earth. And Zedekiah
king of Judah, and his princes I will give into the hand of their
enemies and into the hand of those who seek their lives, into the
hand of the army of the king of Babylon which has withdrawn from
you. Behold, I will command, says the LORD, and will bring them
back to this city; and they will fight against it, and take it, and burn
it with fire. I will make the cities of Judah a desolation without
inhabitant" (34:12-22).

This episode clearly demonstrated to Jeremiah and to anyone
with even the slightest sense of fairness and decency that there was no
moral integrity in anything which the king and his leaders did or said.

Finally, a curious sequence of events occurred which brought
Jeremiah and Zedekiah into close contact again. The series began
when Jeremiah attempted to leave Jerusalem during the period when
the Babylonian siege had been temporarily lifted. He was leaving to
attend to some business in his home in the land of Benjamin (see
37:12). The sentry recognized him and arrested him on the charge of
deserting to the Chaldeans (i.e., the Babylonians). This was a
probable guess on the part of the Jerusalem authorities since
Jeremiah had counseled the people of the city to desert if they wished
to be spared the horrors sure to come. But Jeremiah was no traitor,
and he was not deserting to the enemy. His adversaries never learned
that he had their best interests and the best interests of the people and
the land at heart.

They were angry at Jeremiah for so many reasons and had been
for so long a time that their hostility broke out against the prophet.
They beat him and put him in a dungeon (probably an underground
cellar). Whether he was given anything to eat or drink is not known.
But Jeremiah's life was saved by the curiosity of the weak-willed

Zedekiah who sent for him to ask if there was any word from Yahweh. It is interesting to note that the king, Zedekiah, was so threatened and insecure that he spoke with Jeremiah in secret (see 37:16ff.).

Zedekiah again failed to hear the message he wished to hear, for Jeremiah emphasized that Judah was doomed to fall to Babylon. At this point Jeremiah asked Zedekiah why he was still being treated so cruelly. He referred to the fact that the prophets who had predicted the fall of Babylon were nowhere to be found. They had been discredited and proved to be false. Why then was he still being held? Obviously he thought that he would not be released; therefore, he asked that he not be sent back to the place where he had been. Zedekiah agreed to that request. He did not release the prophet but placed him in a much less confining place and ordered food for him (see 37:20-21).

But the situation was rapidly deteriorating in Judah, and because of that fact the hostility toward Jeremiah continued to grow. The episode recorded in 38:1-6 is thought by some interpreters to be a parallel account of the incident just examined in 37:11-15. But as it is set within the context here, apparently the editor took this to be a different and a subsequent action against Jeremiah. Troubled times produce unusual and sometimes atrocious actions.

Again the weakness of Zedekiah in relation to his princes was manifested. They claimed that Jeremiah was weakening the morale of the soldiers and the people. It is interesting that they asked for the life of Jeremiah; and while the king said that he could not control them, they did not directly execute the prophet. Why they did not is a matter of conjecture. Whether it was because they were afraid to put their hand directly to one who was considered a real prophet of Yahweh or whether they felt that casting him into such a place would be a slower and more agonizing death is not known.

Jeremiah was thrown into an empty cistern with the muck and the mire and the vermin, left to die by starvation and disease. It is no wonder that at times Jeremiah could not control himself and asked Yahweh for vengeance. Perhaps we should note here that in spite of all the cruelties and inhumanity that Jeremiah suffered, he never ceased to continue to speak to these people the message that Yahweh gave him, and he never attempted to take vengeance upon his tormentors himself. True to his promise, however, Yahweh continued to protect Jeremiah in the midst of his sufferings. A servant of the king, who obviously knew about Jeremiah and respected him, begged the king to allow Jeremiah to be taken from the cistern. In a very humane and sensitive way the servant, Ebed-melech, lifted Jeremiah from the mire. He was again placed in the court of the guard.

True to form, Zedekiah sent for Jeremiah once more to ask if Yahweh had a word for him. By this time Jeremiah was weary and somewhat afraid, for he asked the king not to put him to death if he answered. Having received Zedekiah's word (for whatever that was worth!), Jeremiah told him to surrender to the Babylonians. If he did, his life and the lives of many would be spared. But Zedekiah was afraid lest those who had already deserted to the Babylonians would be allowed to kill him. Jeremiah assured him that Yahweh would not allow that to happen. Jeremiah knew the Babylonians very well; in spite of their fierce armies they were fairly enlightened people for such an ancient time. Zedekiah was told plainly, however, that if he did not surrender, he would suffer humiliation and that the city would be burned with fire.

Then Jeremiah said to Zedekiah, "Thus says the Lord, the God of hosts, the God of Israel, If you will surrender to the princes of the king of Babylon, then your life shall be spared, and this city shall not be burned with fire, and you and your house shall live. But if you do not surrender to the princes of the king of Babylon, then this city shall be given into the hand of the Chaldeans, and they shall burn it with fire, and you shall not escape from their hand." King Zedekiah said to Jeremiah, "I am afraid of the Jews who have deserted to the Chaldeans, lest I be handed over to them and they abuse me." Jeremiah said, "You shall not be given to them. Obey now the voice of the Lord in what I say to you, and it shall be well with you, and your life shall be spared. But if you refuse to surrender, this is the vision which the Lord has shown to me: Behold, all the women left in the house of the king of Judah were being led out to the princes of the king of Babylon and were saying,

'Your trusted friends have deceived you
   and prevailed against you;
now that your feet are sunk in the mire,
   they turn away from you.'

All your wives and your sons shall be led out to the Chaldeans, and you yourself shall not escape from their hand, but shall be seized by the king of Babylon; and this city shall be burned with fire" (38:17-23).

After hearing these words from the prophet, Zedekiah asked Jeremiah not to let it be known that he had talked with him. And if anyone should discover that they had conversed, Jeremiah was to say that he was pleading not to be sent back to the house of Jonathan. Unfortunately Zedekiah did not heed Jeremiah's advice. The Babylonians finally took the city and captured Zedekiah attempting to flee to safety. Though the Babylonians often acted in an enlightened manner, they did not hesitate to make examples of those who consistently persisted in rebellion against them. Zedekiah was forced to witness the execution of his sons, whereupon his eyes were put out. He was taken to Babylon in chains. More people were exiled from Judah, and only a few poor were left in the land (see Jeremiah 39:1-10).

Finally, Jeremiah was released from his captivity and given the choice of going to Babylon or remaining in the land. Even though he was assured by the Babylonians that he would be well cared for in that country, Jeremiah chose to remain in the land he loved. By this time, however, we may well wonder how that could be. His loyalty to the land was such that he still felt a call to do all he could for its well-being (see 40:1-6).

To complete the story, Jeremiah did stay in the land which was at that point governed by a certain Gedaliah, whose family had been friends to Jeremiah throughout his career (see 26:24). This man told the people that if they would obey the Babylonians, all would be well with them. But political intrigue does not die easily. There were still those who advocated war with Babylon! There was a plot on Gedaliah's life; and even though he was warned about it, he did not heed the warning. He was assassinated by a man called Ishmael while they ate together (see 40:13–41:3), a horrible breach of Semitic "hospitality." Others were also slain in a senseless act of violence (see 41:4-8). Ishmael and his group were then pursued by a certain Johanan who was a military leader.

Johanan sought the advice of Jeremiah as to what to do, for he feared that the Babylonians would take vengeance on him for what had happened to their appointed governor. Jeremiah counseled them to remain where they were, that the Babylonians would not harm them. If they chose to flee to Egypt, however, he warned that things would not be good for them (see 42:7-22). Alas, after all this time Jeremiah's predictions and counsel had been vindicated, but the people had not yet learned to heed his message. Again they rejected his advice which they had sought, even telling Jeremiah that he was a liar (see 43:1-7)! These leaders then forced a large number of persons to go with them to Egypt, including Jeremiah and Baruch!

While in Egypt Jeremiah continued to declare God's message to the people just as he had before. And the message was not a pleasant one, for the people who came to Egypt accepted Egyptian ways and gods (see 44:1-10). They also again began to worship the "queen of heaven," variously called Astarte or Ishtar, arguing that when the people had worshiped her in the days of Manasseh, no tragedy had come upon the land. Since they stopped, all sorts of evil had befallen them! Jeremiah attempted to tell them that the dark days of evil had come because they had rejected Yahweh and failed to live according to his laws. The "logic" of the people had some validity in terms of sequence of thought but none when it came to the starting point. It was at the basis of their thinking that they were misled from the very beginning. As far as we can determine, this last episode presented here (44:11-30) is the final incident or word known to us from the life and teaching of the prophet Jeremiah.

Questions for Further Study

1. How far should a person of religious conviction go in antagonizing wicked political leaders? How blunt can or should one be in addressing them?

2. Reflect on Jeremiah's sufferings. What did he learn from them? Were they in any way justified? What can we learn from them?

3. Why is it that people who speak the truth realistically are so often ignored, as Jeremiah was, even when events prove they were right?

5
Jeremiah's Relationship with the Religious Leaders

Not only did Jeremiah have his troubles with the political leaders, but he also had difficulties with the religious leaders, both priests and prophets. This is not surprising since he and they were in a sense competing in the same area. Jeremiah's understanding of God and his proclamations about what God was going to do were quite different from the understanding and proclamations of the "orthodox" members of the ecclesiastical establishment.

For a person of such a sensitive nature as Jeremiah's, it was greatly distressing to find not only misunderstanding of God's laws among the religious leaders but also an aggressive and cruel opposition toward anyone who dared to suggest that there could be other interpretations. If one cannot find openness and integrity and a different life-style from the ordinary among those supposedly committed to God's ways, where then could one find such attributes? The diligent search for a man of justice and truth led Jeremiah to the conclusion that there was none to be found.

> Then I said, "These are only the poor,
>   they have no sense;
> for they do not know the way of the LORD,
>   the law of their God.
> I will go to the great,
>   and will speak to them;
> for they know the way of the LORD,
>   the law of their God."

> But they all alike had broken the yoke,
> they had burst the bonds.
> —Jeremiah 5:4-5

Those who were supposed to know the ways of God, to appropriate those laws in their lives, and to challenge the people to accept those laws were themselves as corrupt as if they had never heard of God. They were professional "religionists" whose commitment to religion was only superficial. It was their livelihood, but it was not their life!

Even though Jeremiah spoke out against both the prophets and the priests, there seems to have been more acute animosity between Jeremiah and the prophets than between Jeremiah and the priests. We have already referred to the incident where Pashhur the priest had Jeremiah beaten and placed in stocks for a day and a night (see 20:1ff.). But overall there seem to have been more intense feelings between Jeremiah and the prophets than between Jeremiah and the priests. Whether this was the result of the fact that Jeremiah came from a priestly family or whether it was because Jeremiah as a prophet more directly threatened the prophets cannot be known with precision. That this was the case, however, seems clear enough from a study of the book.

We have already referred to the clash between Jeremiah and Hananiah the prophet over the incident of the yoke (see chapters 27–28). There was, however, a further incident which occurred between Jeremiah and the prophets who had been carried away to Babylon in the first deportation (597 B.C.).

Jeremiah wrote a letter to the exiles (see chapter 29) encouraging them to settle down in Babylon. They were to prepare themselves for a long stay. Obviously there were those there who were predicting that Yahweh would destroy Babylonia and bring the exiles home shortly (see 28:1-4). To that speculation Jeremiah wanted to put an end. Again he had the best interests of the people in mind. For them to settle down and even to pray for the well-being of their captors (see 29:4ff.) would mean a much easier time for them. To be thinking constantly that any time now they would be returning home would place them in a psychological state which would keep them upset and agitated and would ultimately disappoint them to the edge of despair. It could also bring down upon them the wrath of the Babylonians. And Jeremiah also knew that if such a situation developed, the people would blame Yahweh for their misery—as they already were doing! Jeremiah's letter prompted a prophet by the name of Shemaiah to write to the leaders in Jerusalem complaining about the letter. He urged the authorities there to discipline Jeremiah by placing him in the stocks (29:26-27). In response to that attack, Jeremiah sent word to the exiles that Shemaiah was prophesying lies and that neither he nor his descendants would be alive to see the people restored to their land. To speak in such a harsh way was an attempt to demonstrate to the people in exile that they were not to trust in false hopes. Yahweh had no intention of bringing them home soon. It is a curious fact that in spite of the resentment against Jeremiah for his advice, when the people there did what he suggested, they indeed prospered. Some became so prosperous and happy that when they were told they could return to their homeland (*ca.* 538 B.C.), most did not want to leave!

In order to understand some of the negative thoughts that Jeremiah had about the priests and the prophets, and the reasons for those thoughts, it is beneficial to examine several of the passages that reflect the specifics underlying his conclusions.

> "The priests did not say, 'Where is the LORD?'
> Those who handle the law did not know me;
> the rulers transgressed against me;
> the prophets prophesied by Baal,
> and went after things that do not profit."
> —Jeremiah 2:8

Then I said: "Ah, Lord GOD, behold, the prophets say to them, 'You shall not see the sword, nor shall you have famine, but I will give you assured peace in this place.'" And the LORD said to me: "The prophets are prophesying lies in my name; I did not send them, nor did I command them or speak to them. They are prophesying to you a lying vision, worthless divination, and the deceit of their own minds. Therefore thus says the LORD concerning the prophets who prophesy in my name although I did not send them, and who say, 'Sword and famine shall not come on this land': By sword and famine those prophets shall be consumed. And the people to whom they prophesy shall be cast out in the streets of Jerusalem, victims of famine and sword, with none to bury them—them, their wives, their sons, and their daughters. For I will pour out their wickedness upon them" (14:13-16). (Cf. also Jeremiah 4:9-10; 14:17-18.)

These texts indicate that professional "religionists" are not always called by God nor do they always know how to interpret the truth of God for the people whom they have been called to serve. The idea involved here is not so much that they are deliberately evil, as it is that they simply are incapable of knowing what is right and of counseling God's people in the proper way of life. It takes people of sensitivity and insight to serve God; sincerity is not always enough. Not all people who are sincere in their religious faith are capable of being prophets or priests. Some, as the people in Jeremiah's time, learned that fact the hard way!

> An appalling and horrible thing
>   has happened in the land:
> the prophets prophesy falsely,
>   and the priests rule at their direction;
> my people love to have it so,
>   but what will you do when the end comes?
> —Jeremiah 5:30-31

"For from the least to the greatest of them,
    every one is greedy for unjust gain;
and from prophet to priest,
    every one deals falsely.
They have healed the wound of my people lightly,
    saying, 'Peace, peace,'
    when there is no peace.
Were they ashamed when they committed abomination?
    No, they were not at all ashamed;
    they did not know how to blush.
Therefore they shall fall among those who fall;
    at the time that I punish them,
        they shall be overthrown,"
            says the LORD.
                —Jeremiah 6:13-15

"How can you say, 'We are wise,
    and the law of the LORD is with us'?
But, behold, the false pen of the scribes
    has made it into a lie.
The wise men shall be put to shame,

they shall be dismayed and taken;
lo, they have rejected the word of the LORD,
and what wisdom is in them?
Therefore I will give their wives to others
and their fields to conquerors,
because from the least to the greatest
every one is greedy for unjust gain;
from prophet to priest
every one deals falsely.
They have healed the wound of my people lightly,
saying, 'Peace, peace,'
when there is no peace.
Were they ashamed when they committed abomination?
No, they were not at all ashamed;
they did not know how to blush.
Therefore they shall fall among the fallen;
when I punish them, they shall be overthrown,
says the LORD."

—Jeremiah 8:8-12

(See also Jeremiah 18:18.)

In these verses we find Jeremiah speaking of religious leaders who were not simply religiously dull but were downright despicable. The charge here is not that these leaders were incompetent and/or ignorant, but that they were deliberately evil. Two charges seem to appear quite frequently. The first is that the prophets and the priests were primarily interested in "unjust gain," that is, they were more interested in a comfortable position with substantial security than they were in ministering to the real needs of the people.

The second charge is directly related to the first. Because the religious leaders were so interested in a comfortable living, they had no sense of integrity and a complete lack of moral courage. They did the things which they did because the people wanted it to be that way. The people did not want to be upset; they did not want their comfortable lives to be questioned or challenged. They wanted to be reassured that all was well and that all would remain well. But Jeremiah knew that this was not what the people really needed to hear.

When the days of trouble came upon the land, the people needed to be forewarned about what was to take place and why. Otherwise

the lesson that was to be learned, and without which they might have
ultimately perished, would be lost for them.

> my people love to have it so,
>   but what will you do when the end comes?
> —Jeremiah 5:31*b*

Probably the one thing that bothered Jeremiah most in all of this
was the failure of the religious leaders either to recognize realistically
the dangers involved in all that was happening or to have the moral
courage to speak honestly with the people.

> "They have healed the wound of my people lightly,
>   saying, 'Peace, peace,'
> when there is no peace."
> —Jeremiah 6:14

Jeremiah understood the responsibilities that are placed upon a
person called to minister to people in the name of God. It takes
special courage and commitment which the prophets and the priests
of Jeremiah's time simply did not have. But the most sustained
criticism of the religious leaders, specifically the prophets, found in
the Book of Jeremiah is contained in 23:9-40.

> Concerning the prophets:
> My heart is broken within me,
>   all my bones shake;
> I am like a drunken man;
> like a man overcome by wine,
> because of the LORD
>   and because of his holy words.
> For the land is full of adulterers;
>   because of the curse the land mourns,
>   and the pastures of the wilderness are dried up.
> Their course is evil,
>   and their might is not right.
> "Both prophet and priest are ungodly;
>   even in my house I have found their wickedness,
>   says the LORD.
> Therefore their way shall be to them
>   like slippery paths in the darkness,
>   into which they shall be driven and fall;

for I will bring evil upon them
  in the year of their punishment,
    says the LORD.
In the prophets of Samaria
  I saw an unsavory thing:
they prophesied by Baal
  and led my people Israel astray.
But in the prophets of Jerusalem
  I have seen a horrible thing:
they commit adultery and walk in lies;
  they strengthen the hands of evildoers,
  so that no one turns from his wickedness;
all of them have become like Sodom to me,
  and its inhabitants like Gomorrah."
Therefore thus says the LORD of hosts concerning the prophets:
"Behold, I will feed them with wormwood,
  and give them poisoned water to drink;
for from the prophets of Jerusalem
  ungodliness has gone forth into all the land."

Thus says the LORD of hosts: "Do not listen to the words of the
prophets who prophesy to you, filling you with vain hopes; they
speak visions of their own minds, not from the mouth of the LORD.
They say continually to those who despise the word of the LORD, 'It
shall be well with you'; and to every one who stubbornly follows his
own heart, they say, 'No evil shall come upon you.'"

For who among them has stood in the council of the LORD
  to perceive and to hear his word,
  or who has given heed to his word and listened?
Behold, the storm of the LORD!
  Wrath has gone forth,
a whirling tempest;
  it will burst upon the head of the wicked.
The anger of the LORD will not turn back
  until he has executed and accomplished
  the intents of his mind.
In the latter days you will understand it clearly.

"I did not send the prophets,
  yet they ran;
I did not speak to them,

yet they prophesied.
But if they had stood in my council,
then they would have proclaimed my words to my people,
and they would have turned them from their evil way,
and from the evil of their doings.
"Am I a God at hand, says the LORD, and not a God afar off?
Can a man hide himself in secret places so that I cannot see him?
says the LORD. Do I not fill heaven and earth? says the LORD. I have
heard what the prophets have said who prophesy lies in my name,
saying, 'I have dreamed, I have dreamed!' How long shall there be
lies in the heart of the prophets who prophesy lies, and who
prophesy the deceit of their own heart, who think to make my
people forget my name by their dreams which they tell one another,
even as their fathers forgot my name for Baal? Let the prophet who
has a dream tell the dream, but let him who has my word speak my
word faithfully. What has straw in common with wheat? says the
LORD. Is not my word like fire, says the LORD, and like a hammer
which breaks the rock in pieces? Therefore, behold, I am against
the prophets, says the LORD, who steal my words from one another.
    Behold, I am against the prophets, says the LORD, who use
their tongues and say, 'Says the LORD.' Behold, I am against those
who prophesy lying dreams, says the LORD, and who tell them and
lead my people astray by their lies and their recklessness, when I
did not send them or charge them; so they do not profit this people
at all, says the LORD.
    "When one of this people, or a prophet, or a priest asks you,
'What is the burden of the LORD?' you shall say to them, 'You are
the burden, and I will cast you off, says the LORD.' And as for the
prophet, priest, or one of the people who says, 'The burden of the
LORD,' I will punish that man and his household. Thus shall you
say, every one to his neighbor and every one to his brother, 'What
has the LORD answered?' or 'What has the LORD spoken?' But 'the
burden of the LORD' you shall mention no more, for the burden is
every man's own word, and you pervert the words of the living
God, the LORD of hosts, our God. Thus you shall say to the
prophet, 'What has the LORD answered you?' or 'What has the
LORD spoken?' But if you say, 'The burden of the LORD,' thus says
the LORD, 'Because you have said these words, "The burden of the
LORD," when I sent to you, saying, "You shall not say, 'The burden
of the LORD,'"' therefore, behold, I will surely lift you up and cast

you away from my presence, you and the city which I gave to you and your fathers. And I will bring upon you everlasting reproach and perpetual shame, which shall not be forgotten'" (23:9-40).

These verses probably were collected together from several sayings of Jeremiah about the prophets. There are here several charges brought against these religious leaders of Judah. The first is that they were, simply put, immoral. This seems not only to be a reference to their prophesying for gain what the people wished to hear, but it appears that the charge includes also that these men were simply immoral in their living. Jeremiah compared them to the false prophets of the Northern Kingdom of Israel which had fallen in 721 B.C. His hearers would certainly have agreed with him in his assessment of those persons, but they were unable to see that their own religious leaders were just as immoral, if not more so. Jeremiah compared them to those proverbially immoral and corrupt people of Sodom and Gomorrah (23:14)! This was a great evil in the land because the people looked to their religious leaders for moral leadership and example. Jeremiah believed that the ungodliness in the land was at least in part a direct result of the evil of the religious leaders (23:15b).

The next charge (23:16-17) seems to indicate that the prophets simply did not realize or understand what was at stake when they prophesied falsely to the people. They continually told the people that it would be well with them, when, if one simply had the eyes to see, one could understand clearly that things were not "well."

This charge leads to a more serious observation about these prophets (23:18-32). They had not stood in the council of Yahweh; they had not seen a vision of the greatness of God; they simply did not know what the will of God was. Because of these things the prophets deliberately lied! They claimed to have received a revelation through a dream (something that the "genuine" prophets never claimed to have done); because they did not know what to say, they stole oracles from one another. None of these activities on the part of these religious leaders was of any benefit to the people. Again, those charged with responsibility for the people were failing in their duty. Rather than admit that they had not been called, they continued to deceive for their own profit and gain.

The last part of this passage (vv. 33-40) contains another of those famous Semitic word puns. The word is the Hebrew *massa'*, which is translated into the English as "burden." The word play involves the fact that the Hebrew term means basically "something lifted up." The *massa'* then could mean a "burden," but it also could and did refer to a word or message from God, something that was lifted up and became an obligation to both the prophet and the people. What is being said here is that when the people asked for a "word," "message" (burden) from the Lord, Jeremiah was to tell them that *they* were the "burden" upon the Lord. And God would cast off that burden!

The second part of the passage (vv. 34ff.) seems to be a reference to the fact that since the "word" (burden) of the Lord had been for so long perverted and abused by the religious leaders and the people, God commanded the prophets not to speak *massa'* to the people. The people seem to be instructed also not to seek or ask for a message from God. The people and the prophets had for so long spoken their own words and thoughts as God's message that God now forbade them any longer even to say "a burden [message] from the Lord."

This particular idea is one which seems to run through numerous biblical passages. It is the thought that after people for a length of time deliberately and constantly misuse or ignore or pervert the commands or messages from God, they become *incapable* of recognizing them, to say nothing of responding to them. In fact, this is the judgment of God for such deliberate ignoring of his commands. God's judgment is to harden their hearts so as to render them incapable of responding to or even recognizing the message of God. (See Exodus 7–12; Amos 8:11–12; Romans 1:18–32.)

The picture that Jeremiah painted of the religious leaders of his time is a sorry one indeed. They had no real conception as to what was really involved in being a responsible messenger of God and having responsibilities for the people entrusted to their care.

Questions for Further Study

1. What kinds of characteristics does one need in order to be a religious leader? Why?

2. Are there any parallels between some of the religious leaders in history or even today and those persons about whom Jeremiah was talking?

6

Jeremiah's Teaching by Prophetic Signs

Before turning to the spoken teachings of Jeremiah, it is appropriate at this juncture to discuss another method of prophetic teaching. This involved not only the speaking of words, which the people of that time believed had power within them, but also the carrying out of certain acts or "signs." These activities were characteristic of most of the famous prophets and are usually called "prophetic signs." Jeremiah frequently used this method to present his message.

These signs involved an action on the part of the prophet which was believed to have a certain power within it (and which was unleashed by it) to accomplish what the sign depicted. Too often we in these modern times have simply understood these activities as symbols. But to the minds of the ancients these acts were much more than mere symbols. They were part of the accomplishment of the larger act toward which the "sign" pointed. This type of thinking arose from an emphasis in the ancient world on "sympathetic" or "mimetic" magic. This involved the doing of something on a smaller or lower level which would ensure that something be accomplished on a larger or higher level. For example, in the story about Elijah's encounter with the prophets of Baal on Mount Carmel (see 1 Kings 18:20-46), there is such a sign. Unfortunately too often modern persons miss the significance of what was going on.

The question which needed to be settled at that time in Israel was basically that of which God, Yahweh or Baal, was to be worshiped. Since Jezebel was pushing the worship of Baal, the prophets of

Yahweh were being suppressed. The thought was that Yahweh was a war god, a god of the wilderness and of wandering nomads, but Baal was the god of settled people. Baal was a fertility god who sent rain and gave crops, thus insuring the existence of the people. It was at that very point that Elijah challenged the prophets of Baal—he proclaimed that it would not rain again until by Yahweh's word. No one paid him any heed, until two years had elapsed and it had not yet rained!

The story is a familiar one to most students of the Old Testament. The challenge between Baal and Yahweh was engaged. The prophets of Baal called upon their god to answer, but no answer came. When it became Elijah's turn, one notes that he had the altar dedicated to Yahweh saturated with twelve jars of water. Most persons miss the point that the pouring out of the water was a prophetic sign. What was really the test here involved who it was that gave the rain. And the ultimate conclusion of the story shows Yahweh sending the rain. The act of pouring out the water was a "sign" which carried within itself a certain power to accomplish on a larger scale what was being done on the smaller scale.

Now it is obvious that human beings as they are constituted would attempt to use these methods as magical means to manipulate the gods! And many persons in antiquity did. In fact, the earlier use of such signs may have been precisely that—attempts to use the deity for the purposes (some good, some evil) of human agents. But in Israel these signs were interpreted differently. The prophets and the people believed that there was power in these solemn acts which would assist in the accomplishing of the intention of the act. The doing of the act, however, in the prophetic books was at the command of Yahweh, not at the whim of the prophet or the people. In other words the prophet and his action were very definitely a part of the accomplishment of Yahweh's will for the people. This is the reason why the people hated the prophets so intensely when they either proclaimed a message of doom against them or performed a prophetic sign which looked forward to a destructive act by Yahweh against them.

There are other prophetic signs found among the prophets. The names Isaiah gave to his (or others') children were signs for the people of his time (see Isaiah 7:3; 7:10-17; 8:1-4); he walked about the land naked as a sign against reliance upon Egypt (Isaiah 20:1-6)! Hosea's life was in a sense a prophetic sign. He was married to a "woman of harlotry" (Hosea 1:2), and his children were all named as signs for the nation of Israel (see Hosea 1:4-5, 6-7, 8-9). Some of the actions of certain prophets seem rather strange, even weird, to us. Ezekiel especially falls into this category (see Ezekiel 4:1-8; 5:1ff.; 12:1ff.). All of these acts, however, were more than mere symbols to the prophets and to the people for whom and to whom the signs were directed. The prophet Jeremiah also utilized these types of actions to promulgate his teachings. It is perhaps wise to examine these briefly before moving on to his spoken messages.

Thus said the LORD to me, "Go and buy a linen waistcloth, and put it on your loins, and do not dip it in water." So I bought a waistcloth according to the word of the LORD, and put it on my loins. And the word of the LORD came to me a second time, "Take the waistcloth which you have bought, which is upon your loins, and arise, go to the Euphrates, and hide it there in a cleft of the rock." So I went, and hid it by the Euphrates, as the LORD commanded me. And after many days the LORD said to me, "Arise, go to the Euphrates, and take from there the waistcloth which I commanded you to hide there." Then I went to the Euphrates, and dug, and I took the waistcloth from the place where I had hidden it. And behold, the waistcloth was spoiled, it was good for nothing.

Then the word of the LORD came to me: "Thus says the LORD: Even so will I spoil the pride of Judah and the great pride of Jerusalem. This evil people, who refuse to hear my words, who stubbornly follow their own heart and have gone after other gods to serve them and worship them, shall be like this waistcloth, which is good for nothing. For as the waistcloth clings to the loins of a man, so I made the whole house of Israel and the whole house of Judah cling to me, says the LORD, that they might be for me a people, a name, a praise, and a glory, but they would not listen" (13:1-11).

This prophetic sign involves Jeremiah's taking a linen waistcloth (an undergarment worn about the waist which was about mid-thigh in length), which he had worn, and hiding it near a river or body of water. The problem in this verse stems from exactly where Jeremiah put the garment. The Hebrew text reads *PRH* which could mean either Parah, a place not far from Anathoth where there was water, or the Euphrates River. This latter interpretation is the view that most translators take. But if Jeremiah made two trips to the Euphrates

River, that would have required two round trips of over seven hundred miles each. Most commentators believe that the place was at Parah, not the Euphrates.

The real point of the parable is that Yahweh was going to "spoil" Judah as the waistcloth was "spoiled." And the use of the term *PRH* could very well be a word pun so typical of the Hebrew mind. Jeremiah hid the waistcloth in *PRH* (Parah, near his home); the cloth was spoiled there. The place where the people of Judah would be spoiled would be *PRH,* somewhere along the Euphrates where Babylon was!

The waistcloth was used because it covered the loins, and clung to them, one of the most intimate places of a human being. Yahweh made the people of Israel and Judah like a loincloth, to cling to him in an intimate relationship. But they would not listen; therefore they would be spoiled (in fact, Israel already had been).

The interpreter must always keep in mind that to the people of that time Jeremiah's action was more than a symbol. In performing this action (at the command of Yahweh), Jeremiah became an active part of the action which the sign represented. According to that kind of interpretation Jeremiah would be considered by the people as a traitor. The prophets, however, did not perform these signs unless they were convinced that Yahweh had directed them to do so. This is where the Israelite prophets differed from the prophets of other cultures. They would not perform signs simply to accomplish their own goals; they would only perform signs which they were convinced were in agreement with and at the direction of the will of Yahweh.

The word of the LORD came to me: "You shall not take a wife, nor shall you have sons or daughters in this place. For thus says the LORD concerning the sons and daughters who are born in this place, and concerning the mothers who bore them and the fathers who begot them in this land: They shall die of deadly diseases. They shall not be lamented, nor shall they be buried; they shall be as dung on the surface of the ground. They shall perish by the sword and by famine, and their dead bodies shall be food for the birds of the air and for the beasts of the earth. . . .

"And when you tell this people all these words, and they say to you, 'Why has the LORD pronounced all this great evil against us? What is our iniquity? What is the sin that we have committed against the LORD our God?' then you shall say to them: 'Because your fathers have forsaken me, says the LORD, and have gone after other gods and have served and worshiped them, and have forsaken me and have not kept my law, and because you have done worse than your fathers, for behold, every one of you follows his stubborn evil will, refusing to listen to me; therefore I will hurl you out of this land into a land which neither you nor your fathers have known, and there you shall serve other gods day and night, for I will show you no favor'" (16:1-13).

The next prophetic sign is placed within the context of a description of Jeremiah's life, which was basically a lonely existence. This sign is related to the life of the prophet himself. Yahweh commanded Jeremiah not to take a wife or to have children. This was an exceedingly harsh thing for him to accept. In those days it was viewed as natural, even almost obligatory, to marry. And it was especially important to have children, for this assured one of some link or connection with the land of the living after one died and went to Sheol. Therefore, for Jeremiah not to marry as a prophetic sign was a great sacrifice according to the culture of that time.

The sign itself demonstrated to the people the serious nature of what was about to happen. It was, in short, a sign of the conquest of Judah by military defeat. The horrors of war are the same in any generation. People suffer grievous hardships and ignominies; children also are caught up in the suffering; and the dead are left unburied, a terrible disgrace in any time but especially in those days.

What this sign sought to demonstrate to the people was the seriousness of their situation. The normal obligations of life, especially at moments of special sorrow or joy, were inconsequential when weighed against the impending situation for Judah. The sign was given partly to arouse inquisitiveness from the people, to cause them to ask why these things were being contemplated, yea, set in motion against them. To such inquiries Jeremiah was to use the occasion to explain carefully exactly why God was preparing this evil for them. In the background of such an explanation is yet heard the distant call for repentance. But no repentance was forthcoming from these people, as Jeremiah learned to his great sorrow.

Thus said the LORD, "Go, buy a potter's earthen flask, and take some of the elders of the people and some of the senior priests, and go out to the valley of the son of Hinnom at the entry of the

Potsherd Gate, and proclaim there the words that I tell you. You shall say, 'Hear the word of the LORD, O kings of Judah and inhabitants of Jerusalem. Thus says the LORD of hosts, the God of Israel, Behold, I am bringing such evil upon this place that the ears of every one who hears of it will tingle. Because the people have forsaken me, and have profaned this place by burning incense in it to other gods whom neither they nor their fathers nor the kings of Judah have known; and because they have filled this place with the blood of innocents, and have built the high places of Baal to burn their sons in the fire as burnt offerings to Baal, which I did not command or decree, nor did it come into my mind; therefore, behold, days are coming, says the LORD, when this place shall no more be called Topheth, or the valley of the son of Hinnom, but the valley of Slaughter. . . .'

"Then you shall break the flask in the sight of the men who go with you, and shall say to them, 'Thus says the LORD of hosts: So will I break this people and this city, as one breaks a potter's vessel, so that it can never be mended. Men shall bury in Topheth because there will be no place else to bury. Thus will I do to this place, says the LORD, and to its inhabitants, making this city like Topheth. The houses of Jerusalem and the houses of the kings of Judah—all the houses upon whose roofs incense has been burned to all the host of heaven, and drink offerings have been poured out to other gods—shall be defiled like the place of Topheth.'"

Then Jeremiah came from Topheth, where the LORD had sent him to prophesy, and he stood in the court of the LORD's house, and said to all the people: "Thus says the LORD of hosts, the God of Israel, Behold, I am bringing upon this city and upon all its towns all the evil that I have pronounced against it, because they have stiffened their neck, refusing to hear my words" (19:1-15).

Most scholars are agreed that in the episode here cited in chapter 19 two traditions have been put together to form one incident. This is basically an account of a prophetic sign, but added to that is an address by Jeremiah placed here to explain why Yahweh is about to judge the nation as the sign proleptically demonstrates.

Jeremiah was told to take an earthenware flask (probably a water container with a narrow neck) to the Potsherd Gate, and there he was to smash it into pieces. The meaning of the sign was to be that as Jeremiah had smashed the flask into irreparable pieces, so Yahweh would smash the land of Judah and the city of Jerusalem.

The reason for the punishment was the great sin of the people. In the valley of Hinnom (near the Potsherd Gate, according to the editorial comment) the people had sacrificed to other gods. And one of the sacrifices was that of children! ". . . because they have filled this place with the blood of innocents, and have built the high places of Baal to burn their sons in the fire as burnt offerings to Baal, which I did not command or decree, nor did it come into my mind" (19:4b-5).

The conclusion of the episode came when Jeremiah returned to Jerusalem to deliver the message depicted by the sign in the temple. It was this incident that led to the beating of Jeremiah and his placement in the stocks to which we have already referred (see above, pp. 54, 70).

In the beginning of the reign of Zedekiah the son of Josiah, king of Judah, this word came to Jeremiah from the LORD. Thus the LORD said to me: "Make yourself thongs and yoke-bars, and put them on your neck. Send word to the king of Edom, the king of Moab, the king of the sons of Ammon, the king of Tyre, and the king of Sidon by the hand of the envoys who have come to Jerusalem to Zedekiah king of Judah. Give them this charge for their masters: 'Thus says the LORD of hosts, the God of Israel: This is what you shall say to your masters: "It is I who by my great power and my outstretched arm have made the earth, with the men and animals that are on the earth, and I give it to whomever it seems right to me. Now I have given all these lands into the hand of Nebuchadnezzar, the king of Babylon, my servant, and I have given him also the beasts of the field to serve him. All the nations shall serve him and his son and his grandson, until the time of his own land comes; then many nations and great kings shall make him their slave.

""But if any nation or kingdom will not serve this Nebuchadnezzar king of Babylon, and put its neck under the yoke of the king of Babylon, I will punish that nation with the sword, with famine, and with pestilence, says the LORD, until I have consumed it by his hand. So do not listen to your prophets, your diviners, your dreamers, your soothsayers, or your sorcerers, who are saying to you, 'You shall not serve the king of Babylon.' For it is a lie which they are prophesying to you, with the result that you will be removed far from your land, and I will drive you out, and you will perish. But any nation which will bring its neck under the yoke of the king of Babylon and serve him, I will leave on its own land, to till it and dwell there, says the LORD.""

To Zedekiah king of Judah I spoke in like manner: "Bring your necks under the yoke of the king of Babylon, and serve him and his people, and live. Why will you and your people die by the sword, by famine, and by pestilence, as the LORD has spoken concerning any nation which will not serve the king of Babylon? Do not listen to the words of the prophets who are saying to you, 'You shall not serve the king of Babylon,' for it is a lie which they are prophesying to you. I have not sent them, says the LORD, but they are prophesying falsely in my name, with the result that I will drive you out and you will perish, you and the prophets who are prophesying to you" (27:1-15).

In that same year, at the beginning of the reign of Zedekiah king of Judah, in the fifth month of the fourth year, Hananiah the son of Azzur, the prophet from Gibeon, spoke to me in the house of the LORD, in the presence of the priests and all the people, saying, "Thus says the LORD of hosts, the God of Israel: I have broken the yoke of the king of Babylon. Within two years I will bring back to this place all the vessels of the LORD's house, which Nebuchadnezzar king of Babylon took away from this place and carried to Babylon. I will also bring back to this place Jeconiah the son of Jehoiakim, king of Judah, and all the exiles from Judah who went to Babylon, says the LORD, for I will break the yoke of the king of Babylon."

Then the prophet Jeremiah spoke to Hananiah the prophet in the presence of the priests and all the people who were standing in the house of the LORD; and the prophet Jeremiah said, "Amen! May the LORD do so; may the LORD make the words which you have prophesied come true, and bring back to this place from Babylon the vessels of the house of the LORD, and all the exiles. Yet hear now this word which I speak in your hearing and in the hearing of all the people. The prophets who preceded you and me from ancient times prophesied war, famine, and pestilence against many countries and great kingdoms. As for the prophet who prophesies peace, when the word of that prophet comes to pass, then it will be known that the LORD has truly sent the prophet."

Then the prophet Hananiah took the yoke-bars from the neck

of Jeremiah the prophet, and broke them. And Hananiah spoke in the presence of all the people, saying, "Thus says the LORD: Even so will I break the yoke of Nebuchadnezzar king of Babylon from the neck of all the nations within two years." But Jeremiah the prophet went his way.

Sometime after the prophet Hananiah had broken the yoke-bars from off the neck of Jeremiah the prophet, the word of the LORD came to Jeremiah: "Go, tell Hananiah, 'Thus says the LORD: You have broken wooden bars, but I will make in their place bars of iron. For thus says the LORD of hosts, the God of Israel: I have put upon the neck of all these nations an iron yoke of servitude to Nebuchadnezzar king of Babylon, and they shall serve him, for I have given to him even the beasts of the field.'" And Jeremiah the prophet said to the prophet Hananiah, "Listen, Hananiah, the LORD has not sent you, and you have made this people trust in a lie. Therefore thus says the LORD: 'Behold, I will remove you from the face of the earth. This very year you shall die, because you have uttered rebellion against the LORD'" (28:1-17).

We have already examined this episode in the life of Jeremiah in another context (see above, pp. 61f.), but as one can readily see, the basis of the account centers in one of those prophetic signs. As a sign to Zedekiah and the people (this incident obviously occurred soon after the first exile in 597 B.C.) that they should serve the Babylonians and not bring further distress upon themselves by rebelling, Jeremiah wore wooden yoke-bars on his neck. His message was to the point. Yahweh had decreed that the nation should serve Nebuchadnezzar. They and the exiles needed to accept that fact; if they did, things would go well for them.

But there was almost constant agitation on the part of the pro-Egyptian faction in the land urging rebellion against Babylonia. Some of the prophets were caught up in this furor also, either by conviction or by false hope that somehow God would destroy Babylonia and restore the fortunes of the land. Hananiah was one of those prophets. He predicted that Yahweh would break the yoke of Nebuchadnezzar and that within two years all the exiles and the vessels taken from the temple would be returned to the land of Judah. It was a fine hope, but it was very unrealistic, smacking too much of the fairy-tale ending of "living happily ever after."

It is interesting that Jeremiah himself hoped that Hananiah's prophecy would be correct! But he could not be convinced that this would occur. In his own heart he was certain that his understanding was right. And he simply said to Hananiah and the people that the "proof will be in the pudding." When the allotted time had come, it would be clearly seen who was right.

This kind of situation must have posed quite a problem for the people of that day, especially those who were really sensitive to what was right and to the word that Yahweh wished for them to hear. Two prophets (or one prophet and a group of prophets) were prophesying exactly opposite messages, both in the name of Yahweh! In such a situation how could one know which was the *true* prophet of God? The prophets who ultimately were designated as "true" prophets emphasized that their understanding of the present situation and the immediate future which would arise out of that situation was determined by their understanding of the nature of God as previously revealed to Israel. This revelation had taken place in two sections: the first was the way Yahweh had acted before in relationship with his people; and the second was his revelation through the Law given at the time of the covenant mediated by Moses. The principles and personality of God which evolved from these previous occasions became the foundational props by which a true and sensitive person could, if one really wished, determine the ways and will of God for any moment. The true prophets then were realists, not starry-eyed dreamers who simply wished out loud.

Hananiah then performed a prophetic sign of his own, breaking the yoke-bars which Jeremiah was carrying around. But his sign was of no avail. If Yahweh had not commanded the sign, it carried no power within itself. It is interesting that Jeremiah went away for a period of time after Hananiah broke his yoke. Whether he did this because he was angry or frustrated or even afraid is not certain. In all probability it was to meditate on the events which had transpired and to await some word from God. That word came and it instructed him to proclaim that Yahweh would replace the wooden yoke with one of iron. Whether Jeremiah actually came forward with an iron yoke is not stated in the text, but in the light of the usual methods of operation of the prophets it is quite likely that he did.

Jeremiah also predicted that Hananiah would die within a year—and he did!

Jeremiah said, "The word of the LORD came to me: Behold,

Hanamel the son of Shallum your uncle will come to you and say, 'Buy my field which is at Anathoth, for the right of redemption by purchase is yours.' Then Hanamel my cousin came to me in the court of the guard, in accordance with the word of the LORD, and said to me, 'Buy my field which is at Anathoth in the land of Benjamin, for the right of possession and redemption is yours; buy it for yourself.' Then I knew that this was the word of the LORD.

"And I bought the field at Anathoth from Hanamel my cousin, and weighed out the money to him. . . . 'For thus says the LORD of hosts, the God of Israel: Houses and fields and vineyards shall again be bought in this land'" (32:6-15). (Cf. also Jeremiah 32:24-25 and vv. 42-44.)

The next sign is one that should have brought hope to the people of Judah. Jeremiah was approached by one of his kinsmen, Hanamel, and asked to buy a piece of property which belonged to his family. When this happened, Jeremiah was under arrest in the court of the guard, but he interpreted this approach as a message from Yahweh. He bought the land, therefore, as a sign that some day the people would be restored to their land, that normal activities would again be resumed.

Interspersed within this story is another of the explanations by the Deuteronomic editors as to why the exile took place. The sayings are quite Jeremianic, but the placing of the material together here in this way is the result of the editorial process.

By this acted parable Jeremiah was fulfilling the stipulation of his call, both to destroy and to build, to pluck up and to plant (see 1:10).

The word which came to Jeremiah from the LORD in the days of Jehoiakim the son of Josiah, king of Judah: "Go to the house of the Rechabites, and speak with them, and bring them to the house of the LORD, into one of the chambers; then offer them wine to drink." So I took Ja-azaniah the son of Jeremiah, son of Habazziniah, and his brothers, and all his sons, and the whole house of the Rechabites. I brought them to the house of the LORD into the chamber of the sons of Hanan the son of Igdaliah, the man of God, which was near the chamber of the princes, above the chamber of Ma-aseiah the son of Shallum, keeper of the threshold. Then I set before the Rechabites pitchers full of wine, and cups; and

I said to them, "Drink wine." But they answered, "We will drink no wine, for Jonadab the son of Rechab, our father, commanded us, 'You shall not drink wine, neither you nor your sons for ever; you shall not build a house; you shall not sow seed; you shall not plant or have a vineyard; but you shall live in tents all your days, that you may live many days in the land where you sojourn.' We have obeyed the voice of Jonadab the son of Rechab, our father, in all that he commanded us, to drink no wine all our days, ourselves, our wives, our sons, or our daughters, and not to build houses to dwell in. We have no vineyard or field or seed; but we have lived in tents, and have obeyed and done all that Jonadab our father commanded us. But when Nebuchadrezzar king of Babylon came up against the land, we said, 'Come, and let us go to Jerusalem for fear of the army of the Chaldeans and the army of the Syrians.' So we are living in Jerusalem."

Then the word of the LORD came to Jeremiah: "Thus says the LORD of hosts, the God of Israel: Go and say to the men of Judah and the inhabitants of Jerusalem, Will you not receive instruction and listen to my words? says the LORD. The command which Jonadab the son of Rechab gave to his sons, to drink no wine, has been kept; and they drink none to this day, for they have obeyed their father's command. I have spoken to you persistently, but you have not listened to me. I have sent to you all my servants the prophets, sending them persistently, saying, 'Turn now every one of you from his evil way, and amend your doings, and do not go after other gods to serve them, and then you shall dwell in the land which I gave to you and your fathers.' But you did not incline your ear or listen to me. The sons of Jonadab the son of Rechab have kept the command which their father gave them, but this people has not obeyed me. Therefore, thus says the LORD, the God of hosts, the God of Israel: Behold, I am bringing on Judah and all the inhabitants of Jerusalem all the evil that I have pronounced against them; because I have spoken to them and they have not listened, I have called to them and they have not answered."

But to the house of the Rechabites Jeremiah said, "Thus says the LORD of hosts, the God of Israel: Because you have obeyed the command of Jonadab your father, and kept all his precepts, and done all that he commanded you, therefore thus says the LORD of hosts, the God of Israel: Jonadab the son of Rechab shall never lack a man to stand before me" (35:1-19).

The incident described in this passage probably occurred about 600–598 B.C. when the Babylonian army was marauding in the land of Judah but was not yet quite prepared to begin the final siege of Jerusalem. Jehoiakim was still king at the time.

Jeremiah was told to go to the community of the Rechabites, bring them to the temple, and offer them wine to drink. This group of people was a small sect within Israelite religion which evolved from its founder, a certain Jonadab (Jehonadab) ben Rechab (see 2 Kings 10:15-17). This group adhered quite vigorously to the traditions of the nomadic past, believing that the new ways had corrupted the worship of Yahweh. They did not believe in owning property, living in houses, or having any association with the "fruit of the vine," especially wine. The only reason they were at this time within Jerusalem was that there were military problems in the land. Otherwise they lived basically as nomadic shepherds.

Jeremiah used these persons of integrity as a sign against the people of Judah to demonstrate that people can and do keep commitments and obligations. They were not supposed to drink wine; and when offered wine, they quickly refused. This episode should not be interpreted to mean that Jeremiah was a Rechabite or even agreed with their ideas. Obviously he did not, since he lived in a city, dwelt in a house, and later bought a piece of property. What he did admire in these people was their commitment to do what they believed was right and to keep the traditions that had been handed on to them.

The people of Judah who had been possessors of so much more than the Rechabites had failed miserably in keeping their commitments to God and in guarding their religious traditions. The message was that the people of Judah would be judged, but the Rechabites would always have someone from among them to stand before God. Jeremiah obviously admired this group of people immensely.

During the period of turmoil between the first deportation in 598–597 B.C. and the second in 587–586, there was much intrigue and political manipulation occurring. In the midst of this period Zedekiah had to go to Babylonia to assure Nebuchadnezzar that he was loyal and part of no rebellious scheme to turn against him.

On the occasion of that visit Jeremiah gave to someone whom he trusted (Baruch's brother) a scroll. The contents of the scroll were supposed to have been an account of what was to happen to Babylonia later. After all, even though that nation was being used by

God to accomplish his purposes, it nevertheless was wicked and evil. And therefore the day of judgment would come for the people of Babylonia as surely as it had for others. It would have to, since according to Jeremiah, there would come a day when the people of Judah could be free to return to their homeland.

The scroll was to be read aloud upon reaching Babylon (presumably not in the presence of Zedekiah, who would probably have misinterpreted it), and then it was to be weighted down with a rock and thrown into the Euphrates River. The sign would then await its fulfillment in Yahweh's own time and by his own direction of history. (For this episode, see Jeremiah 51:59-64.)

We recall that Jeremiah was forced to accompany the group which fled to Egypt. Upon his arrival in Egypt Jeremiah performed another prophetic sign. He took two large stones and buried them before the government building in the city Tahpanhes. This was to demonstrate that Egypt would be subject to the rule of Babylonia, the stones being the sign that the Babylonian throne would rest upon them. (See Jeremiah 43:8-13.)

As far as we know, Babylonia never really defeated Egypt in such a way as to rule completely over that country. It was not until 568–567 that Nebuchadnezzar invaded Egypt, and we simply do not know exactly how that encounter concluded. That Babylonia was the dominant power in the world of that time was certain, however, and Jeremiah's sign held true at least that far.

Questions for Further Study

1. What do you think of the prophetic "signs"? Even though we do not think of such activities in the same way as the people of that period did, are there occasions when actions similar to those of Jeremiah could make an impression where words would not? Can you think of any such possibilities?

2. Can you think of any groups today similar to the Rechabites? Do they have anything to teach the more "traditional" people? What?

7
Jeremiah's Concept of Sin

It is in examining his oracles (basically included in chapters 1–25) that one learns what a magnificent poet the prophet Jeremiah was. His marvelous expression and the flowing quality of his poetry are rarely matched within the writings of the Old Testament. We have already discussed the characteristics of Hebrew poetry and examined some of Jeremiah's teachings; but as we turn now to investigate more closely the principle teachings of this great and sensitive man, we see very clearly just how talented a poet he was.

The Nature of Sin

Apart from his understanding of Yahweh and his commandments, Jeremiah's basic religious understandings arose from his conception of the nature of sin. What was wrong with the world and people's relationship with God and with one another was a direct result of the pervasive nature of sin in the human race. Jeremiah meditated long about this matter, as one can see by the reading of the entire book. He came to the painful conclusion that sin was a part of the very fabric and fiber of human nature. His most frequently heard lament was that relating to the perverseness of the human heart. Over and over again he pled with the people to change the direction of their lives, and one of the more graphic figures he used was that of "circumcising [i.e., cleansing] their hearts" (see 4:4a). It is in the unrepentant heart, the heart untouched by God's law and mercy, that evil finds its conception and a fertile place for multiplication.

Note two passages where Jeremiah emphasized this idea:

The heart is deceitful above all things;
and desperately corrupt;
who can understand it?
"I the LORD search the mind and try the heart,
to give to every man according to his ways,
according to the fruit of his doings."

—Jeremiah 17:9-10

"How can you say, 'I am not defiled,
I have not gone after the Baals'?
Look at your way in the valley;
know what you have done—
a restive young camel interlacing her tracks,
a wild ass used to the wilderness,
in her heat sniffing the wind!
Who can restrain her lust?
None who seek her need weary themselves;
in her month they will find her.
Keep your feet from going unshod
and your throat from thirst.
But you said, 'It is hopeless,
for I have loved strangers,
and after them I will go.'"

—Jeremiah 2:23-25

It is because of the "deceitful heart" that human beings are so sinful. By nature they, like the wild ass, seek out that which they "desire." But somehow in addition to a "natural" sinfulness, people by their own deliberate choices intensify evil. Jeremiah was throughout his ministry constantly and continuously amazed at the stupidity of humans in their intensification of evil.

Declare this in the house of Jacob,
proclaim it in Judah:
"Hear this, O foolish and senseless people,
who have eyes, but see not,
who have ears, but hear not.
Do you not fear me? says the LORD;
Do you not tremble before me?
I placed the sand as the bound for the sea,

a perpetual barrier which it cannot pass;
though the waves toss, they cannot prevail,
   though they roar, they cannot pass over it.
But this people has a stubborn and rebellious heart;
   they have turned aside and gone away.
They do not say in their hearts,
   'Let us fear the LORD our God,
who gives the rain in its season,
   the autumn rain and the spring rain,
and keeps for us
   the weeks appointed for the harvest.'
Your iniquities have turned these away,
   and your sins have kept good from you.
For wicked men are found among my people;
   they lurk like fowlers lying in wait.
They set a trap;
   they catch men.
Like a basket full of birds,
   their houses are full of treachery;
therefore they have become great and rich,
   they have grown fat and sleek.
They know no bounds in deeds of wickedness;
   they judge not with justice
the cause of the fatherless, to make it prosper,
   and they do not defend the rights of the needy.
Shall I not punish them for these things?
      says the LORD,
   and shall I not avenge myself
on a nation such as this?"

               —Jeremiah 5:20-29
           (See also Jeremiah 2:9-13.)

All of this leads to one conclusion. Evil is such an integral part of the human scene and it is intensified so much by the added dimension of human stupidity that God no longer seems real. People come to trust solely and directly in humankind as the epitome of all knowledge and hope. This is a horrible mistake.

     Thus says the LORD:
     "Cursed is the man who trusts in man

and makes flesh his arm,
   whose heart turns away from the LORD.
He is like a shrub in the desert,
   and shall not see any good come.
He shall dwell in the parched places of the wilderness,
   in an uninhabited salt land.

"Blessed is the man who trusts in the LORD,
   whose trust is the LORD.
He is like a tree planted by water,
   that sends out its roots by the stream,
and does not fear when heat comes,
   for its leaves remain green,
and is not anxious in the year of drought,
   for it does not cease to bear fruit."
          —Jeremiah 17:5-8
          (See Psalm 1.)

Perhaps, however, some of the most graphic and, in some sense, beautiful of Jeremiah's poetic oracles are seen in his depiction of the intensity of the sin of the people of God. These were people who should have known better, people whose lives had been touched and changed (in the past at least) by the hand of God, people who had been given directions and instructions for a truly good life. But these people had refined sin in such a way that its intensity was multiplied manyfold.

"For long ago you broke your yoke
   and burst your bonds;
   and you said, 'I will not serve.'
Yea, upon every high hill
   and under every green tree
   you bowed down as a harlot.
Yet I planted you a choice vine,
   wholly of pure seed.
How then have you turned degenerate
   and become a wild vine?
Though you wash yourself with lye and use much soap,
   the stain of your guilt is still before me,
      says the Lord GOD."
          —Jeremiah 2:20-22

"And if you say in your heart,
    'Why have these things come upon me?'
    it is for the greatness of your iniquity
    that your skirts are lifted up,
    and you suffer violence."
                                                    —Jeremiah 13:22

"As a well keeps its water fresh,
    so she keeps fresh her wickedness;
violence and destruction are heard within her;
    sickness and wounds are ever before me."
                                                    —Jeremiah 6:7

"You shall say to them, Thus says
        the LORD:
When men fall, do they not rise again?
    If one turns away, does he not return?
Why then has this people turned away
    in perpetual backsliding?
They hold fast to deceit,
    they refuse to return.
I have given heed and listened,
    but they have not spoken aright;
no man repents of his wickedness,
    saying, 'What have I done?'
Every one turns to his own course,
    like a horse plunging headlong into battle.
Even the stork in the heavens knows her times;
    and the turtledove, swallow, and crane
    keep the time of their coming;
but my people know not
    the ordinance of the LORD."
                                                    —Jeremiah 8:4-7

"The sin of Judah is written with a pen of iron; with a point of
diamond it is engraved on the tablet of their heart, and on the horns
of their altars, while their children remember their altars and their
Asherim, beside every green tree, and on the high hills, on the
mountains in the open country. Your wealth and all your treasures
I will give for spoil as the price of your sin throughout all your

territory. You shall loosen your hand from your heritage which I gave to you, and I will make you serve your enemies in a land which you do not know, for in my anger a fire is kindled which shall burn for ever" (17:1-4). (See also Jeremiah 2:33-35.)

These passages demonstrate just how far into a state of sinfulness the people of Judah had sunk. As the leopard by nature has spots and the Ethiopian a dark skin, the people of Judah by nature were sinful to the core. Their sin was written by means of a pen of iron with a diamond point upon the hardened tablets of their heart. Not even the strongest lye (or bleach) could cleanse these people. They were so immoral that their immorality seemed to be regimented.

> "How can I pardon you?
>   Your children have forsaken me,
>   and have sworn by those who are no gods.
> When I fed them to the full,
>   they committed adultery
>   and trooped to the houses of harlots.
> They were well-fed lusty stallions,
>   each neighing for his neighbor's wife.
> Shall I not punish them for these things?
>   says the LORD;
>   and shall I not avenge myself
>   on a nation such as this?"
>   —Jeremiah 5:7-9

The humor of this (and other prophetic) passages is sometimes missed because of the serious nature of the situation. There are, however, many really humorous oracles within the prophetic literature which illustrate the intensity of the people's evil natures.

Jeremiah used other means also to illustrate his point. He urged a thorough search of the city of Jerusalem to find just one righteous person.

> Run to and fro through the streets of Jerusalem,
>   look and take note!
> Search her squares to see
>   if you can find a man,
> one who does justice

and seeks truth;
that I may pardon her.
Though they say, "As the LORD lives,"
yet they swear falsely.
O LORD, do not thy eyes look for truth?
Thou hast smitten them,
but they felt no anguish;
thou hast consumed them,
but they refused to take correction.
They have made their faces harder than rock;
they have refused to repent.

Then I said, "These are only the poor,
they have no sense;
for they do not know the way of the LORD,
the law of their God.
I will go to the great,
and will speak to them;
for they know the way of the LORD,
the law of their God."
But they all alike had broken the yoke,
they had burst the bonds.

—Jeremiah 5:1-5

He moved first among the "common" people and found none. But he realized that perhaps he was looking in the wrong place. He then searched among the leaders, the ones whose business it was to know about such things and to act justly and fairly. Alas, not even among those who were supposed to be different could one just person be found.

Not even judgment had caused any change. In the biblical traditions the judgment of God was not so much for God's benefit, to allow him to "get even" for the sins of humanity. Rather, judgment was always for the express purpose of causing repentance. Most often when judgment is mentioned, it referred to a partial judgment, sent by God to stir people to turn away from their wickedness. (See Amos 4:6-11; Revelation 6:1-8; 9:20-21, for just a few examples.) This kind of judgment was often viewed as similar to the refining fire which separated the precious metal from the worthless minerals surrounding it. So too Jeremiah viewed God's judgment in this way, but the people still were not able to see in their trials the hand of God acting for their ultimate redemption.

Some of the evil deeds of the nation have already been discussed in previous sections. It is well to mention again, however, that these people were sacrificing children (see 7:30-31) to pagan gods. We are also reminded of the grossly hypocritical action which transpired during the siege of Jerusalem when the slaves were released and freed. And when the Babylonian army had to leave momentarily to deal with the Egyptians, this order was rescinded (see 34:8ff.). This was a time when no one could trust anyone else. There can never be any possibility for a good life for anyone unless people can basically trust other people. But in the land of Judah at that moment of history, no one could trust anyone!

> Let every one beware of his neighbor,
>   and put no trust in any brother;
> for every brother is a supplanter,
>   and every neighbor goes about as a slanderer.
> Every one deceives his neighbor,
>   and no one speaks the truth;
> they have taught their tongue to speak lies;
>   they commit iniquity and are too weary to repent.
> Heaping oppression upon oppression,
>   and deceit upon deceit,
>   they refuse to know me, says the LORD.
>   —Jeremiah 9:4-6

Jeremiah saw clearly the great tragedy in all this, however. It was not necessary for these people to have to live this way. Those were miserable times, but help was near at hand if only they would reach out and accept it. Jeremiah's famous saying speaks directly to that point.

> My grief is beyond healing,
>   my heart is sick within me.
> Hark, the cry of the daughter of my people
>   from the length and breadth of the land:
> "Is the LORD not in Zion?
>   Is her King not in her?"
> "Why have they provoked me to anger with their graven

images, and with their foreign idols?"
"The harvest is past, the summer is ended,
and we are not saved."
For the wound of the daughter of my people is my heart wounded,
I mourn, and dismay has taken hold on me.
Is there no balm in Gilead?
Is there no physician there?
Why then has the health of the daughter of my people
not been restored?

—Jeremiah 8:18-22

For those who are not aware of the fact, Gilead was famous in those days for its medicine (which it either made or distributed by trade from elsewhere). The figure that Jeremiah paints so graphically here is similar to a modern situation in which a dying person refuses to take the antibiotic which will effect a rapid recovery. There definitely was a balm in Gilead, but the people refused to take it!

There is in the prophetic teachings (and in the biblical teachings overall) the idea that even though God is slow to anger, plenteous in mercy, and forgives sin, there does come a point at which all that ends. Even though God sends partial judgments in order to cause people to repent, if these do not produce the desired results, there comes a time of ultimate judgment. In other words, there is a point of no return in the life of an individual or group or institution or nation. There comes a place where turning back is either impossible or useless! Macbeth of Shakespeare's play learned that. His schemes and plots and evil had led him to a point in his life where he could say:

"I am in blood,
stept in so far, that, should I wade no more,
Returning were as tedious as go o'er."
(Macbeth, Act III, Scene IV)

He had learned the hard lesson that there is a point of no return.

Jeremiah taught the same idea many years ago to the people of Judah. Those persons had gone so far with their sin that Jeremiah says not even the two most famous "intercessors" (Moses and Samuel) in the history of Israel could be of any assistance to them. (See Exodus 32:11-14, 30-32; Numbers 14:13-24; Deuteronomy 9:13-19, 25-29; 1 Samuel 7:8f; 12:19-23; Psalm 99:6-8.)

Then the LORD said to me, "Though Moses and Samuel stood before me, yet my heart would not turn toward this people. Send them out of my sight, and let them go!" (15:1).

Finally, God even commanded Jeremiah not to pray on behalf of the people anymore. It is surprising that Jeremiah could or would want to pray for these people, considering the manner in which they had treated him. But obviously he had been doing precisely that. Now God says that he must not do that any longer.

The LORD said to me: "Do not pray for the welfare of this people. Though they fast, I will not hear their cry, and though they offer burnt offering and cereal offering, I will not accept them; but I will consume them by the sword, by famine, and by pestilence" (14:11-12). (See also Jeremiah 11:14-17.)

Jeremiah had a great deal to say about human sinfulness and God's response to it. That human nature changes very little through the millennia of history is quite obvious. One sees the same attitudes and mistakes prevalent even today!

Questions for Further Study

1. How do the figures for sin in the Book of Jeremiah correspond to the sinful nature of the people of Judah? Where could such figures appropriately be used in today's society? Can you think of figures that would be more appropriate for today?

2. Discuss the idea that there comes a time when it may be too late to repent. Is this a result of God's harshness or the result of human nature? Give some examples from history and present society to illustrate the point.

8
Jeremiah's Concept of God and Covenant

His Understanding of Yahweh

It is always difficult to attempt to describe one's own understanding of God, to say nothing of describing someone else's experience. But since the Book of Jeremiah contains so many very intimate "conversations" between Jeremiah and God, it would be unthinkable not to say a few words about Jeremiah's understanding of the nature of Yahweh.

Perhaps the most fundamental point to be made in relation to this concept is that Jeremiah viewed and understood Yahweh as a Person with whom he could and did have a close relationship. Yahweh "knew" Jeremiah, and Jeremiah "knew" Yahweh. As already noted, the verb "to know" in the Old Testament usually carries the connotation of a close, intimate relationship between persons. This is what Jeremiah experienced in his life, a relationship so close that he could even "converse" with God.

It is interesting in reading through the oracles of Jeremiah to see the different role relationships that Jeremiah experienced with God. At some points the relationship of Yahweh to Jeremiah is almost like that of a parent, at other points like a supportive friend, and at still others an adversary relationship. But throughout there is a personal, experiential dimension of which Jeremiah was always cognizant.

While a great deal of Jeremiah's close association with and understanding of God comes from the "confessions," it is still appropriate to cite a few texts to illustrate the points referred to above.

> "Before I formed you in the womb I knew you,
>   and before you were born I consecrated you;
> I appointed you a prophet to the nations."
> > —Jeremiah 1:5

> But the LORD said to me,
> "Do not say, 'I am only a youth';
>   for to all to whom I send you you shall go,
> and whatever I command you you shall speak."
> > —Jeremiah 1:7

"And I, behold, I make you this day a fortified city, an iron pillar, and bronze walls, against the whole land, against the kings of Judah, its princes, its priests, and the people of the land. They will fight against you; but they shall not prevail against you, for I am with you, says the LORD, to deliver you" (1:18-19).

> Why is my pain unceasing,
>   my wound incurable,
>   refusing to be healed?
> Wilt thou be to me like a deceitful brook,
>   like waters that fail?
> > —Jeremiah 15:18

> O LORD, thou hast deceived me,
>   and I was deceived;
> thou art stronger than I,
>   and thou hast prevailed.
> I have become a laughingstock all the day;
>   every one mocks me.
> For whenever I speak, I cry out,
>   I shout, "Violence and destruction!"
> For the word of the LORD has become for me
>   a reproach and derision all day long.
> > —Jeremiah 20:7-8

There is one final note about Jeremiah's understanding of the nature of Yahweh. To Jeremiah he was Lord of history and life, individually and collectively. God is a "Person" but more than a person; he is Creator of all. Therefore everything should be in proper awe of him. "Great" and "majestic" are two adjectives that can be used to illustrate Jeremiah's thoughts about the God who was so real to him.

> There is none like thee, O Lord;
>> thou art great, and thy name is great in might.
> Who would not fear thee, O King of the nations?
>> For this is thy due;
> for among all the wise ones of the nations
>> and in all their kingdoms
>> there is none like thee.
> They are both stupid and foolish;
>> the instruction of idols is but wood!
> Beaten silver is brought from Tarshish,
>> and gold from Uphaz.
> They are the work of the craftsman
>> and of the hands of the goldsmith;
>> their clothing is violet and purple;
>> they are all the work of skilled men.
> But the Lord is the true God;
>> he is the living God and the everlasting King.
> At his wrath the earth quakes,
>> and the nations cannot endure his indignation.
>> —Jeremiah 10:6-10

> It is he who made the earth by his power,
>> who established the world by his wisdom,
>> and by his understanding stretched out the heavens.
> When he utters his voice there is a tumult of waters
>> in the heavens,
>> and he makes the mist rise from the ends of the earth.
> He makes lightnings for the rain,
>> and he brings forth the wind from his storehouses.
>> —Jeremiah 10:12-13

His Understanding of the Covenants and the Exiles

Even though Jeremiah was convinced that the exile was the will of Yahweh, and justly so, because of the sin of the people, the question that still needed to be answered concerned that of Yahweh's promises to Moses and David. When those covenants were made, the people believed that they were to be everlasting. The Northern Kingdom, Israel, had already passed into oblivion. And now it appeared that Judah could easily follow that same route. What was one to make of these new possibilities in the light of the old promises?

The first and most prominent teaching of Jeremiah relating to the Mosaic covenant (which was still considered basic to the life of the nation) was that the covenant Yahweh made with Israel contained certain conditions. To be sure, God had made promises to the people, and it was assumed that human beings could not keep perfectly *all* the conditions. After all, the people were frail; God alone was all-powerful. But too often the people found it very easy to rely upon the greatness of God and the magnitude of his mercy. It was too easy to excuse themselves, because they were "only" human, from keeping their part of the covenant agreement. But the prophets in general and Jeremiah in particular taught that the people were expected to keep the precepts of the covenant. Privilege begets responsibility (see Amos 3:2). Those who have experienced and received good things from God were expected to keep their part of the bargain. If they did not, serious consequences were certain to come upon them. In short then, the teaching of the prophets was that Yahweh was not failing to keep his promises and to live up to the covenant obligations, but the people were. How then could they be surprised at what was happening? The events that were about to transpire were directly the result of their own failure to do what they were obligated to do.

There are several passages in the Book of Jeremiah which speak directly to that point.

> Hear the word of the LORD, O house of Jacob, and all the families of the house of Israel. Thus says the LORD:
> "What wrong did your fathers find in me
>   that they went far from me,
> and went after worthlessness, and became worthless?
> They did not say, 'Where is the LORD
>   who brought us up from the land of Egypt,
> who led us in the wilderness,
>   in a land of deserts and pits,
> in a land of drought and deep darkness,
>   in a land that none passes through,
>   where no man dwells?'

And I brought you into a plentiful land
to enjoy its fruits and its good things.
But when you came in you defiled my land,
and made my heritage an abomination."
                                    —Jeremiah 2:4-7

The word that came to Jeremiah from the LORD: "Hear the words of this covenant, and speak to the men of Judah and the inhabitants of Jerusalem. You shall say to them, Thus says the LORD, the God of Israel: Cursed be the man who does not heed the words of this covenant which I commanded your fathers when I brought them out of the land of Egypt, from the iron furnace, saying, Listen to my voice, and do all that I command you. So shall you be my people, and I will be your God, that I may perform the oath which I swore to your fathers, to give them a land flowing with milk and honey, as at this day." Then I answered, "So be it, LORD."

Again the LORD said to me, "There is revolt among the men of Judah and the inhabitants of Jerusalem. They have turned back to the iniquities of their forefathers, who refused to hear my words; they have gone after other gods to serve them; the house of Israel and the house of Judah have broken my covenant which I made with their fathers. Therefore, thus says the LORD, Behold, I am bringing evil upon them which they cannot escape; though they cry to me, I will not listen to them. Then the cities of Judah and the inhabitants of Jerusalem will go and cry to the gods to whom they burn incense, but they cannot save them in the time of their trouble. For your gods have become as many of your cities, O Judah; and as many as the streets of Jerusalem are the altars you have set up to shame, altars to burn incense to Baal" (11:1-5, 9-13).

The same principle held true for the Davidic covenant (see 2 Samuel 7:8-16; 23:5). Even though Yahweh made the covenant with David and his house (dynasty), the same types of obligations were incumbent upon the ruler as were binding upon the people. If the kings broke the covenant agreements, Yahweh was no longer bound to his part. And there are in the Book of Jeremiah many incidents and oracles which show just how far the rulers had gone in ignoring their covenant obligations (see 21:10–23:4).

"And to the house of the king of Judah say, 'Hear the word of

the LORD, O house of David! Thus says the LORD:
> "'Execute justice in the morning,
>> and deliver from the hand of the oppressor
>> him who has been robbed,
>
> lest my wrath go forth like fire,
>> and burn with none to quench it,
>> because of your evil doings.'"

Thus says the LORD: "Go down to the house of the King of Judah, and speak there this word, and say, 'Hear the word of the LORD, O King of Judah, who sit on the throne of David, you, and your servants, and your people who enter these gates. Thus says the LORD: Do justice and righteousness, and deliver from the hand of the oppressor him who has been robbed. And do no wrong or violence to the alien, the fatherless, and the widow, nor shed innocent blood in this place. For if you will indeed obey this word, then there shall enter the gates of this house kings who sit on the throne of David, riding in chariots and on horses, they, and their servants, and their people. But if you will not heed these words, I swear by myself, says the LORD, that this house shall become a desolation.

"'And many nations will pass by this city, and every man will say to his neighbor, "Why has the LORD dealt thus with this great city?" And they will answer, "Because they forsook the covenant of the LORD their God, and worshiped other gods and served them"'" (21:11-12; 22:1-5, 8-9).

There are two passages at least which give hope for the future of the Davidic house, however. As Jeremiah thought that at some later time the exiles would be allowed to return home, so he also thought that there would be a Davidic representative to rule over them.

"Behold, the days are coming, says the LORD, when I will raise up for David a righteous Branch, and he shall reign as king and deal wisely, and shall execute justice and righteousness in the land. In his days Judah will be saved, and Israel will dwell securely. And this is the name by which he will be called: 'The LORD is our righteousness'" (23:5-6).

"Behold, the days are coming, says the LORD, when I will fulfil the promise I made to the house of Israel and the house of Judah. In those days and at that time I will cause a righteous Branch to spring forth for David; and he shall execute justice and righteousness in the land. In those days Judah will be saved and Jerusalem will dwell securely. And this is the name by which it will be called: 'The LORD is our righteousness.'

"For thus says the LORD: David shall never lack a man to sit on the throne of the house of Israel, and the Levitical priests shall never lack a man in my presence to offer burnt offerings, to burn cereal offerings, and to make sacrifices for ever" (33:14-17).

The passage in chapter 33 just cited is not found in the Greek translation of the Hebrew Old Testament. Some have conjectured, therefore, that the passage is a later addition to the Book of Jeremiah. That question is not one that should bother us at the moment, but a related one is important. Some have argued that the passage as it is presented represents an absolute guarantee by Yahweh to restore the Davidic dynasty and the Levitical priesthood in the temple for all time. While the statement is made positively here (whether by Jeremiah or a later Deuteronomic editor is irrelevant), it must be remembered that no promises are made by God unequivocally but are *always contingent on the response of the people involved.* To interpret the passage otherwise would be to go against the basic and clear teachings of the remainder of the entire Book of Jeremiah. There was definite hope for restoration. (That restoration did, in fact, come.) But the length of the restoration was always understood to be contingent upon how the people kept the terms of the covenant!

Questions for Further Study

1. Can people today still experience God as a Person as Jeremiah did? How can this be? In thinking about one's own relationship with God, could you share some experience with others?

2. Why is it important to understand that a covenant is a two-way agreement? Can you think of ways in our society today in which people think of God's grace as only "one way," i.e., toward people, with no responsibility on their part? What happens to human relationships when covenants are not kept on both sides? Examples?

3. Can historical events today (as the exile in Jeremiah's time) be interpreted as an act of God for a purpose? Can you think of any in history? Any that may be imminent today?

9
The Place of Hope in Jeremiah's Teaching

We have discussed already (see above, pp. 17ff.) the older view that all the preexilic prophets were prophets of doom, while hope passages must be assigned to the postexilic prophets. There is some truth in the generalization, but the categories cannot be pressed too rigidly on the material contained within the prophetic books. Each passage espousing hope found in a preexilic prophet must, however, be carefully examined to determine if that saying is historically set within the prophet's time and if that saying is in alignment in style and content with the other sayings of the prophet agreed to be authentic.

This procedure should be applied also to the hope passages which are found in the Book of Jeremiah. But even though Jeremiah was basically a preexilic prophet, he prophesied at the very moment of the exile. This means that he was in reality a transitional prophet, bridging the gap between the preexilic messages of doom and the exilic and postexilic messages of comfort and hope. So it will not be surprising to find more genuine hope passages in this book than in some of the other preexilic prophets.

Jeremiah's hope seems to center on two basic ideas. First, and he shared this with all the prophets, there was hope if the people would truly repent. Yahweh is a God of mercy, who forgives sins, who is slow to anger. But no superficial, external "form" can be substituted by the people for real religious change. Most of the prophets are very adamant at this point, and this can be clearly discerned in Amos (cf. 5:21-24), Hosea (cf. 6:6), and Isaiah (cf. 1:12-17). Jeremiah, too, found some faint glimmer of hope for the people, *if* they would truly repent. Repentance in the biblical texts means much more, however, than merely feeling sorrow or confessing sins. It means a change in direction, a turning away from one life-style and embracing another, totally different one in a close, intimate relationship with God. And no sin is too great for God to forgive—if one truly repents.

> "If you return, O Israel,
>   says the LORD,
> to me you should return.
> If you remove your abominations from my presence,
>   and do not waver,
> and if you swear, 'As the LORD lives,'
>   in truth, in justice, and in uprightness,
> then nations shall bless themselves in him,
>   and in him shall they glory."

For thus says the LORD to the men of Judah and to the inhabitants of Jerusalem:

> "Break up your fallow ground,
>   and sow not among thorns.
> Circumcise yourselves to the LORD,
>   remove the foreskin of your hearts,
>   O men of Judah and inhabitants of Jerusalem;
> lest my wrath go forth like fire,
>   and burn with none to quench it,
>   because of the evil of your doings."
>   —Jeremiah 4:1-4

One notes, however, that there are serious consequences involved if one does not truly repent! And the people of Judah did not repent!

> "I have given heed and listened,
>   but they have not spoken aright;
> no man repents of his wickedness,
>   saying, 'What have I done?'
> Every one turns to his own course,
>   like a horse plunging headlong into battle."
>   —Jeremiah 8:6

The second basis for hope, and really the only one that held any possibility for the people of Judah, was Jeremiah's firm belief that God could and would make a way for a new beginning. This new beginning would be based on the goodness of God and a changed heart within the people. The basic text for this understanding of Jeremiah's is found in the famous story in which Jeremiah saw a potter at work. From his observation of this common everyday event Jeremiah learned a great lesson about God.

> The word that came to Jeremiah from the LORD: "Arise, and go down to the potter's house, and there I will let you hear my words." So I went down to the potter's house, and there he was working at his wheel. And the vessel he was making of clay was spoiled in the potter's hand, and he reworked it into another vessel, as it seemed good to the potter to do.
>
> Then the word of the LORD came to me: "O house of Israel, can I not do with you as this potter has done? says the LORD. Behold, like the clay in the potter's hand, so are you in my hand, O house of Israel. If at any time I declare concerning a nation or a kingdom, that I will pluck up and break down and destroy it, and if that nation, concerning which I have spoken, turns from its evil, I will repent of the evil that I intended to do to it. And if at any time I declare concerning a nation or a kingdom that I will build and plant it, and if it does evil in my sight, not listening to my voice, then I will repent of the good which I had intended to do to it. Now, therefore, say to the men of Judah and the inhabitants of Jerusalem: 'Thus says the LORD, Behold, I am shaping evil against you and devising a plan against you. Return, every one from his evil way, and amend your ways and your doings.'
>
> "But they say, 'That is in vain! We will follow our own plans, and will every one act according to the stubbornness of his evil heart'" (18:1-12).

Jeremiah learned from this incident that even though a piece of clay may be "spoiled" in the potter's hand, the potter is able nevertheless to make something useful of it. He found hope here that even yet God could use the spoiled clay of Judah. The passage concludes with another call to repentance which the people of Judah again rejected. The fact that the people still refused to repent made it clear to Jeremiah that judgment had to come. But there was still hope for the future, not a hope that resided in humankind but a hope that was firmly centered in the plans and purposes of God. Yahweh remained the potter for all nations!

The hope that Jeremiah saw, oddly enough, was the exile! While the nation at that time looked upon the exile as the end of all their hopes and dreams (and to a certain extent it was), that very judgment of God contained the seeds of hope for a new beginning. There are three basic passages that speak to this point.

"Therefore thus says the LORD of hosts: Because you have not obeyed my words, behold, I will send for all the tribes of the north, says the LORD, and for Nebuchadrezzar the king of Babylon, my servant, and I will bring them against this land and its inhabitants, and against all these nations round about; I will utterly destroy them, and make them a horror, a hissing, and an everlasting reproach. Moreover, I will banish from them the voice of mirth and the voice of gladness, the voice of the bridegroom and the voice of the bride, the grinding of the millstones and the light of the lamp. This whole land shall become a ruin and a waste, and these nations shall serve the king of Babylon seventy years. Then after seventy years are completed, I will punish the king of Babylon and that nation, the land of the Chaldeans, for their iniquity, says the LORD, making the land an everlasting waste. I will bring upon that land all the words which I have uttered against it, everything written in this book, which Jeremiah prophesied against all the nations. For many nations and great kings shall make slaves even of them; and I will recompense them according to their deeds and the work of their hands" (25:8-14).

This warning by Jeremiah to the people is located at the conclusion of the first collection of Jeremiah's oracles. The last part of this section (vv. 13b-14) may be a part of the editorial revision that took place at the time when the portions of tradition were welded together to form the book as we now have it. We recall from our introductory comments that in the Greek version the oracles against foreign nations stood after 25:13a.

Those are problems that are of secondary concern to us, however, in this study. The point that Jeremiah made is that Judah would surely go into an exile that would last for a long period of time, seventy years. The figure seventy was probably not meant to be taken literally but rather interpreted as a very long period of time. Jeremiah would use the figure again in another context (see 29:10). What he was attempting to make clear was that the nation of Judah would, for a long period of time, cease to exist. There was hope, however, that, after the period was completed, Yahweh would return the people to their land.

> After Nebuchadrezzar king of Babylon had taken into exile from Jerusalem Jeconiah the son of Jehoiakim, king of Judah, together with the princes of Judah, the craftsmen, and the smiths, and had brought them to Babylon, the LORD showed me this vision: Behold, two baskets of figs placed before the temple of the LORD. One basket had very good figs, like first-ripe figs, but the other basket had very bad figs, so bad that they could not be eaten. And the LORD said to me, "What do you see, Jeremiah?" I said, "Figs, the good figs very good, and the bad figs very bad, so bad that they cannot be eaten."
>
> Then the word of the LORD came to me: "Thus says the LORD, the God of Israel: Like these good figs, so I will regard as good the exiles from Judah, whom I have sent away from this place to the land of the Chaldeans. I will set my eyes upon them for good, and I will bring them back to this land. I will build them up, and not tear them down; I will plant them, and not uproot them. I will give them a heart to know that I am the LORD; and they shall be my people and I will be their God, for they shall return to me with their whole heart.
>
> "But thus says the LORD: Like the bad figs which are so bad they cannot be eaten, so will I treat Zedekiah the king of Judah, his princes, the remnant of Jerusalem who remain in this land, and those who dwell in the land of Egypt. I will make them a horror to all the kingdoms of the earth, to be a reproach, a byword, a taunt, and a curse in all the places where I shall drive them. And I will send sword, famine, and pestilence upon them, until they shall be utterly destroyed from the land which I gave to them and their fathers" (24:1-10).

The second of these passages is rooted in one of those common, ordinary, everyday scenes from which the prophet with his "spiritual eye" could see a revelation of God. In this instance Jeremiah saw two baskets of figs, one containing good figs and the other containing figs that had spoiled or rotted. Since this incident took place between 597 and 586, Jeremiah naturally sought to find a meaning that would be applicable to that moment of history.

In reflecting upon the situation, Jeremiah came to understand that the basket of good figs which were useful and for which there was some hope represented the exiles in Babylon. This was true not because the people who had been carried away were "good," but because from that group Jeremiah saw hope for the future of the nation. It was among them that Yahweh would act so that the nation might some day be restored to its place in God's plan for the world.

The bad figs, however, represented the people who were left in the land, especially Zedekiah and his zealous, but stupid, advisers. Through them there was no hope for the nation of Judah. They were bad figs! Jeremiah realized that those persons would be ultimately destroyed by their blind and futile opposition to the great nation of Babylonia.

These are the words of the letter which Jeremiah the prophet sent from Jerusalem to the elders of the exiles, and to the priests, the prophets, and all the people, whom Nebuchadnezzar had taken into exile from Jerusalem to Babylon. . . . It said: "Thus says the LORD of hosts, the God of Israel, to all the exiles whom I have sent into exile from Jerusalem to Babylon: Build houses and live in them; plant gardens and eat their produce. Take wives and have sons and daughters; take wives for your sons, and give your daughters in marriage, that they may bear sons and daughters; multiply there, and do not decrease. But seek the welfare of the city where I have sent you into exile, and pray to the LORD on its behalf, for in its welfare you will find your welfare. For thus says the LORD of hosts, the God of Israel: Do not let your prophets and your diviners who are among you deceive you, and do not listen to the dreams which they dream, for it is a lie which they are prophesying to you in my name; I did not send them, says the LORD.

"For thus says the LORD: When seventy years are completed for Babylon, I will visit you, and I will fulfil to you my promise and bring you back to this place. For I know the plans I have for you, says the LORD, plans for welfare and not for evil, to give you a future and a hope. Then you will call upon me and come and pray to me, and I will hear you. You will seek me and find me, when you seek me with all your heart, I will be found by you, says the LORD, and I will restore your fortunes and gather you from all the nations and all the places where I have driven you, says the LORD, and I will bring you back to the place from which I sent you into exile" (29:1-14).

Jeremiah then wrote a letter to the people who were in exile in Babylon. It is interesting to note that in this letter he referred to the people who remained behind in Judah as "vile figs" (see 29:17). The purpose of the letter was to encourage the people there not to lose heart or to be misled by false hopes.

His basic message was that they would remain in Babylon for a long period of time, at least two generations. The figure of seventy years was probably only meant to be an approximation to show that the people presently in captivity would *not* come home, but that the return would not be postponed forever. In other words, their children and grandchildren would be among those who would return. The people were, therefore, urged to pray for the welfare of Babylon! For Jeremiah there was a very practical reason to do that. The people of Judah who were residing there were an integral part of that society. If Babylon fared well, so would they.

He admonished them not to be led astray by false prophets mistakenly predicting that Yahweh would release them soon to return home. Jeremiah called these persons "deceivers," people who spoke lies in the name of God. The counsel which the great prophet gave to the people was similar to his own understanding of God's relationship with himself. They were unhappy and in the midst of enemies. But if they would trust in Yahweh, they would survive and even prosper!

Most of Jeremiah's "hope" is contained, however, in chapters 30–31 (perhaps 32–33 should also be added) which many scholars designate the "Book of Consolation." In all probability these two portions, 30–31 and 32–33, were originally separate, the former containing oracles of hope and the latter containing the same theme but set within a biographical account. In the final editing of the book they were put together into a single unit by the device of "common theme." Since we have already discussed those incidents of 32–33, we shall concentrate here on chapters 30–31.

It is at this point that the reader should be reminded again of the problems related to "hope" passages within the preexilic prophetic books. Since the basic message before the exile was doom, hope had to come from the exile and beyond. But while there may be some points at which the later editors incorrectly inserted hope passages into the preexilic prophetic sayings (see especially Amos 9:8c-15), it would be quite unrealistic to deny any hope to the preexilic prophets. Their understanding of Yahweh and his greatness would certainly not allow them to be so myopic. Especially is this true with Jeremiah. The relationship which he had with God and his understanding of him could not be contained in one single idea or set of ideas. Yahweh, being the kind of God that he is, has plans and designs for the future which will include a place for his people. Therefore, there must be hope centered in the very existence of God.

It is quite possible that the majority of the passages contained in 30–31 were originally collected together in a "book" by themselves. To that collection an introduction was added (see 30:1-3) for the purpose of setting the stage for the ideas contained within the oracles. The message is that of the restoration of the people of God.

One further problem should be mentioned before turning directly to the text of these chapters. This problem relates to the question of what Jeremiah meant when he used the term "Israel." Was he referring to the old Northern Kingdom and its restoration? Or was he using the term in a collective sense referring to the *unified* people of God? One recalls that the two nations had been together for only a short period of time and were severed about 922 B.C. First, Israel had gone into exile in 721 B.C. and at this point Judah was in the process of having the same fate befall her. What Jeremiah hoped for was a return to the land of a unified people of God who could indeed be designated by the old title, "Israel" of God. In other words what Jeremiah hoped for was not necessarily a return of the Northern tribes (they were gone), but a resettlement of the land by the people of God once more. Whether the prophet really had in mind the specific return of the Northern tribes (as some scholars argue) is uncertain. To this interpreter, however, it seems highly unlikely.

These are the words which the LORD spoke concerning Israel and Judah:
"Thus says the LORD:
We have heard a cry of panic,
    of terror, and no peace.
Ask now, and see,
    can a man bear a child?
Why then do I see every man

with his hands on his loins like a woman in labor?
Why has every face turned pale?
Alas! that day is so great
there is none like it;
it is a time of distress for Jacob;
yet he shall be saved out of it.

"And it shall come to pass in that day, says the LORD of hosts,
that I will break the yoke from off their neck, and I will burst their
bonds, and strangers shall no more make servants of them. But
they shall serve the LORD their God and David their king, whom I
will raise up for them" (30:4-9).

This oracle (along with 30:12-17) seems to set the context for the
remaining oracles of hope, because these verses describe the horror of
the judgment that has come upon the people of God for their
wickedness. Verses 8-9 and 16-17 begin to set the pattern of hope
which will be delineated more specifically in the material that follows.
It seems clear that the editors who arranged the material wanted to
make certain that there was absolutely no question that the tragedy of
the exiles was a direct result of the sin of the people. But Yahweh
planned a restoration of their health! And those who had ridiculed
the name of God because of the destruction of his nation would learn
by the harsh reality of experience that he had been in control of all
that had happened.

Supposedly both the people of God and the peoples of the world
would learn through the "hindsight of history" that there was a
purpose in the events that had transpired.

Behold the storm of the LORD!
Wrath has gone forth,
a whirling tempest;
it will burst upon the head of the wicked.
The fierce anger of the LORD will not turn back
until he has executed and accomplished
the intents of his mind.
In the latter days you will understand this.
—Jeremiah 30:23-24

The remaining portions of these chapters all seem to be primarily directed toward the understanding that God would bring the exiles back and restore a nation in the land. There are several passages which some scholars feel reflect the content and style of that great prophet of the exile whose poetic excellence is preserved in Isaiah 40–55. Some even go so far as to postulate that these passages of Jeremiah were composed in the light of that tradition. It is beyond our intentions here to argue the pros and cons of that possibility. Suffice it to say that it is possible for later traditions to have crept into the large mass of material remembered as from Jeremiah. But it is also possible that some of Jeremiah's teaching could very well have influenced later prophetic circles. The passages which fall into this category are the following:

> "Then fear not, O Jacob my servant,
>> says the LORD,
>> nor be dismayed, O Israel;
> for lo, I will save you from afar,
>> and your offspring from the land of their captivity.
> Jacob shall return and have quiet and ease,
>> and none shall make him afraid.
> For I am with you to save you,
>> says the LORD;
> I will make a full end of all the nations
>> among whom I scattered you,
>> but of you I will not make a full end.
> I will chasten you in just measure,
>> and I will by no means leave you unpunished."
>> —Jeremiah 30:10-11

> "Hear the word of the LORD, O nations,
>> and declare it in the coastlands afar off;
> say, 'He who scattered Israel will gather him,
>> and will keep him as a shepherd keeps his flock.'
> For the LORD has ransomed Jacob,
>> and has redeemed him from hands too strong for him.
> They shall come and sing aloud on the height of Zion,
>> and they shall be radiant over the goodness of the LORD,
> over the grain, the wine, and the oil,
>> and over the young of the flock and the herd;
> their life shall be like a watered garden,

and they shall languish no more.
Then shall the maidens rejoice in the dance,
    and the young men and the old shall be merry.
I will turn their mourning into joy,
    I will comfort them, and give them gladness for sorrow.
I will feast the soul of the priests with abundance,
    and my people shall be satisfied with my goodness,
                says the LORD."
                    —Jeremiah 31:10-14 (See also 31:7-9.)

Whatever the source of these passages (and it must be said that there are numerous points where Jeremianic ideas are indeed prominent), they describe in a magnificent way the hope and joy that will be attendant to the return from exile and the reestablishment of the nation of God's people.

In addition to this "grouping" there is another which scholars have observed. The passages involved are 31:2-6 and 31:15-22. Most interpret these passages as belonging to a very early period in Jeremiah's ministry when he hoped for and envisioned a restoration of the nation, both of Judah and Israel. This could have come from the historical background described in 2 Kings 23:15-20 and 2 Chronicles 34:6f. when Josiah attempted to expand the territory of Judah into the area of the old Northern Kingdom.

Even though Jeremiah does refer quite specifically to the northern area where Israel once existed, it seems too strained to argue that Jeremiah, realist that he was, was actually envisioning the return of the northern exiles. It seems best to understand Jeremiah's comments in the passages here as references to his hope that one day Yahweh would bring the exiles from Babylon back to Judah. And having done so, he would then make of them (if they would allow him to do so!) a great nation once again, populating and controlling the old area which once belonged to the united kingdom of David and Solomon.

Since the Hebrew people believed in the idea of "corporate personality," i.e., the idea that all members of the group both past and future were present in the existence of the group at any moment in history, Jeremiah would in all probability understand the restoration of the people in the land as a restoration of "Israel," the united people of God. It is not really necessary to understand these passages as early simply because they refer to Israel or to the northern areas. And it is not necessary either to understand the references to the restoration of the united people of God as a specific concept involving a literal return of the long ago exiled Israelites. It is interesting that Ezekiel thinks in much the same kinds of categories (see Ezekiel 37:11-28, for example). What Jeremiah, and later Ezekiel, did envision was a restored people of God, unified in the land that once belonged to them. This unified people of God would be to their way of thinking a genuine restoration of Israel.

> Thus says the LORD:
> "The people who survived the sword
>   found grace in the wilderness;
> when Israel sought for rest,
>   the LORD appeared to him from afar.
> I have loved you with an everlasting love;
>   therefore I have continued my faithfulness to you.
> Again I will build you, and you shall be built
>   O virgin Israel!
> Again you shall adorn yourself with timbrels,
>   and shall go forth in the dance of the merrymakers.
> Again you shall plant vineyards
>   upon the mountains of Samaria,
> the planters shall plant,
>   and shall enjoy the fruit.
> For there shall be a day when watchmen will call
>   in the hill country of Ephraim:
> 'Arise, and let us go up to Zion,
>   to the LORD our God.'"
>
> —Jeremiah 31:2-6

"Behold, the days are coming, says the LORD, when I will sow the house of Israel and the house of Judah with the seed of man and the seed of beast. And it shall come to pass that as I have watched over them to pluck up and break down, to overthrow, destroy, and bring evil, so I will watch over them to build and to plant, says the LORD. In those days they shall no longer say:

> 'The fathers have eaten sour grapes,
>   and the children's teeth are set on edge.'

But every one shall die for his own sin; each man who eats sour grapes, his teeth shall be set on edge" (31:27-30).

The remaining teachings of these two chapters contain basically passages of hope for the restoration of God's people in a new community. It seems best to concentrate on two passages, 30:18-22 and 31:31-34, for these passages give a sensitive insight into the essence of God's compassion and will for his people and into Jeremiah's own shining hope in the midst of the almost unbearable circumstances of his own life.

"Thus says the LORD:
Behold, I will restore the fortunes of the tents of Jacob,
    and have compassion on his dwellings;
the city shall be rebuilt upon its mound,
    and the palace shall stand where it used to be.
Out of them shall come songs of thanksgiving,
    and the voices of those who make merry.
I will multiply them, and they shall not be few;
    I will make them honored, and
        they shall not be small.
Their children shall be as they were of old,
    and their congregation shall be established before me;
    and I will punish all who oppress them.
Their prince shall be one of themselves,
    their ruler shall come forth from their midst;
I will make him draw near, and he shall approach me,
    for who would dare of himself to approach me?
        says the LORD.
And you shall be my people,
    and I will be your God."
                                        —Jeremiah 30:18-22

"Behold, the days are coming, says the LORD, when I will make a new covenant with the house of Israel and the house of Judah, not like the covenant which I made with their fathers when I took them by the hand to bring them out of the land of Egypt, my covenant which they broke, though I was their husband, says the LORD. But this is the covenant which I will make with the house of Israel after those days, says the LORD: I will put my law within them, and I will write it upon their hearts; and I will be their God, and they shall be my people. And no longer shall each man teach his neighbor and each his brother, saying, 'Know the LORD,' for they shall all know me, from the least of them to the greatest, says the LORD; for I will forgive their iniquity, and I will remember their sin no more" (31:31-34).

The first of these texts is a moving poetic description of life in a community where "peace," well-being, is again the normal order. People quite often become tired of the ordinary and routine in life; but when it is taken away, how they long to have it as it was! This is a picture of "how it was" restored. And the basis for that kind of hope lies in the sure belief of Jeremiah that,

> "And you shall be my people,
> and I will be your God."
> —Jeremiah 30:22

The second passage is, of course, one that is familiar to many persons. It is the "New Covenant" passage. Scholars argue about whether this teaching originally belonged to Jeremiah or whether it was a later addition from some other prophetic tradition. The fact that the elements in the passage are quite Jeremianic and because this particular concept is really not found anywhere else among the prophetic writings leads this interpreter to the conclusion that the teaching definitely originated with Jeremiah.

It is also worth noting that even though the RSV does not place the new covenant "elements" in poetic form, it surely seems to fit the poetic style.

> "I will put my law within them,
> and I will write it upon their hearts.
> And I will be their God,
> and they shall be my people.
> And no longer shall each man teach his neighbor
>   and each his brother, saying, 'Know the LORD,'
> for they shall all know me,
> from the least of them to the greatest.
> For I will forgive their iniquity,
> and I will remember their sin no more."
> —Jeremiah 31:33b-34

There are a number of points that can and should be made about this crucial passage. First of all, it must be emphasized that Jeremiah is not, as most of the older commentators argued, the great prophet of individualism. The older interpreters viewed Old Testament religion as basically corporate or collective, as Yahweh making his covenant with the nation. They held that this was a lower stage of religious development which later evolved into the higher stage where God deals with individuals. In the biblical tradition, however, neither the group nor the individual has a monopoly on "pride of place" in relationship with God. To be sure, the earlier traditions do seem to emphasize the corporate nature of religion while the later traditions emphasize the individual. But in neither are the two emphases separate and singular. The individual in the older times was important especially as that person contributed to or brought shame upon the group of which she or he was a member. And in the later period the individual is never really free to do totally what is pleasing to oneself, but that person always is responsible to the group to support it and build it up.

Having said this, we see immediately in the new covenant passage that this covenant is to be made not with individuals *per se* but with the "house of Israel and the house of Judah." Therefore in spite of the emphasis found in older commentaries on Jeremiah as the great prophet of individualism, on closer examination we find here the old emphasis on God's covenant with a people. But the two elements of individualism and the corporate group are held together in a healthy tension. Both are considered important.

What, then, are the "new" elements in Jeremiah's new covenant? Basic to this covenant is Jeremiah's emphasis on the fact that the old covenant broke down at the point that the requirements of that agreement were external to the people. This new relationship with God would be based not upon precepts written down upon tablets of stone but rather upon the tablets of the hearts of the people. The precepts would become a part of the very nature of their being. As the old nature could not be changed by externals (see 13:23), the new nature would be made possible by God's instruction and purposes written upon the hearts of the people. The "heart" is usually designated as the place of purpose and will; therefore when one changes the heart, one changes the direction of the person's life.

A second feature of the new covenant lies in the fact that all people (at least those within the new covenant community) would "know" Yahweh. As already pointed out, "to know" means "to have an intimate personal relationship with." All the people of the new community would "know" God; and there would be no need for anyone to teach others, for Yahweh would be known from the least to the greatest of them. This seems to be closely related to Jeremiah's experience earlier in his ministry when he searched for a good person, only to find that they were all corrupt from the least to the greatest (see 5:1-5).

The third feature seems to be a new emphasis also. This covenant would not be based on any foundation other than the mercy of God which will forgive the sins of the people. Human beings cannot stand in the proper relationship with anyone unless others are willing to forgive them for what they are and to accept them for what they are. Yahweh was willing to do exactly that and to offer to the people a new opportunity of relationship with himself. No relationship, human or otherwise, can fail to affect a human personality. Those whom we know and encounter influence us either for good or for ill. There is no neutrality in a relationship that is truly meaningful. So too with one's relationship with God. If God forgives one's sins, there stands open the possibility of opportunities for growth and experiences that alone were never within grasp. A relationship with God like that described by Jeremiah can change an individual radically, and the change of individuals can change the nature and character of the group.

Biblically speaking, both the individual and the group are important. Jeremiah's own life reflected the importance of a close, individual, personal relationship with God. But that relationship needs the support of others who are experiencing the same kind of commitment. And each person contributes to the "planting and building" (see 1:10) of the group so that the whole becomes greater than the sum of its parts. Jeremiah really longed for a new community in which each person would be a contributing and important factor and in which the group would support its members. Perhaps it was because he never had any such support that he hoped for it so keenly.

The new community that Jeremiah envisioned would be a group of people who had God's law written upon their hearts. And every person would know Yahweh because God would forgive the people's sins and transform them into persons who could accomplish more than they ever dreamed, both individually and collectively.

Questions for Further Study

1. Why is it that even in proclamations of judgment the proph-

ets can find some cause for hope?

2. Can you think of instances where God has brought genuine good from an evil situation?

3. Reflect upon Jeremiah's famous "new covenant" passage. How has it been used in other contexts? What can it mean for us today?

10
The Relevance of Jeremiah for Our Times

Problems are always encountered when one attempts to transport the teachings and message directed to one particular time and place into a different time and place. This is especially true for the Jewish and Christian devotee of today, both of whom believe that the books of the Hebrew Scriptures are authoritative for life now.

All too often we find two rather popular approaches to this problem. One holds that the writings of the biblical books speak directly and precisely to our times just as they did to the time of the inspired spokesmen of God. All we need do is to take the verses and apply them directly to persons or institutions today for them to be applicable. There are moments when we would very much like to do exactly that, especially with the teachings of the prophets when someone or something is acting very much out of accord with righteousness, justice, and truth (as we see it).

The second approach holds that what is necessary is to extract principles or guidelines from the study of the biblical literature. These then can be applied to any situation where the interpreter thinks it will fit. What happens, all too often, in such an approach is that the principles become so generalized that they are also neutralized! One talks so much about "principles" and seeks so diligently to find them that they never are specifically applied.

What is needed, if one can define such a procedure, is to combine the "principle" approach with the "direct" approach in such a way that the principles can be applied specifically to concrete historical situations presently encountered which approximate as much as possible the concrete historical situations which originally called forth the teaching. This is certainly not an easy procedure. And as with the prophets of Jeremiah's day, some persons will interpret the historical context and the application of the religious principles involved in one manner; and some others will interpret the same data differently. The answer to the question of who is correct in his or her interpretation and application may have to await the verdict of history.

Even though the task is not an easy one nor are the results certain, it nevertheless behooves those who do hold that the Scriptures are relevant for present society and life to get with the difficult job of applying the teachings of the Bible to life. Otherwise the biblical collection becomes simply another book of antiquity which means nothing for present living except to satisfy one's curiosity about how things were "back then."

Upon turning to explore some possibilities for discussion and application, one must say in all candor that not all people will agree with either the interpretation or the application of the texts and principles involved. Not all will agree with the specific issues cited for discussion, for it must be admitted that issues are much more alive when they are "pressing" in a particular time and place.

The issues that will be discussed in relation to Jeremiah's teaching are: the problem of the nature of sin; the problem of the relationship of a religious person and the state, including a brief look at one's view toward foreign nations; and the concept of hope both personal and corporate in the light of the nature of God.

The primary problem that always plagues the human race is sin. One need only to read the books of history and the daily paper or even look around in one's everyday existence to know that evil, sin, or whatever one wishes to call it is a constant companion of the human race. What causes it, and what can be done about it? Jeremiah speaks to that problem, and his beautiful poetic descriptions of the nature of sin are at points just as appropriate now as they were then.

Sin arises from a perverted heart. The will of human beings is misdirected and misguided. It is set upon its own way to be accomplished by its own devices. To Jeremiah, sin was not an external force which caused people to do things they really would not have done otherwise. The common cry of moderns is "I am caught in a web not of my own making and am, therefore, helpless to resist." Or to put it more humorously, "The devil made me do it!" The prophet

Jeremiah would certainly not agree with that assessment.

There has been for a number of years now a reluctance to talk about sin, because somehow to admit that sin exists makes one responsible for one's actions. But the prophet Jeremiah certainly felt that people, individually and collectively, are responsible for their actions. It is interesting that it has taken one of the country's leading psychologists, Dr. Karl Menninger, to remind the religious community that sin is indeed alive and well among and within the human race.[1]

According to Jeremiah, sin is rooted in the human heart, the place where human will and volition reside. People do deliberately sin, thinking that in such activity they are finding the true meaning and pleasures of life. One is reminded of Jeremiah's famous description of the men of Judah marching as an army battalion to the houses of ill repute or the description of each one as an overheated stallion neighing for his neighbor's wife! (see 5:7-8). In some respects sin does not change at all.

All of this, however, has come from the perverted "heart" of human beings (see 17:9). What is needed is an action on God's part which will dramatically and drastically change the heart so that the law of God is by nature part and parcel of it. Jeremiah looks forward, as we have seen, to a time when God would do just that. Whatever else one might wish to say about sin, to the mind of Jeremiah it is *the* fundamental problem of the human race. God takes sin seriously and acts against it. Human beings should consider its seriousness and its consequences also. To refuse to do so is to invite disaster both individually and corporately. Jeremiah believed that God could and would forgive sin, for the purpose of creating a new beginning for the person or nation. This forgiveness was not cheap, however, but it required an acceptance of and a commitment to the terms of the new covenant which were imposed by God.

A second topic which can well be a basis for discussion arising from Jeremiah's experience and teaching concerns that of the relationship between a religious person and the state. It is in relation to this topic that many feel the application of the biblical teachings, especially the prophetic teaching, can be made directly. They feel that as the prophets stood "eyeball to eyeball" with the king, defiantly and at great risk to themselves condemning immoral behavior on the part

[1] Karl Menninger, *Whatever Became of Sin?* (New York: Hawthorn Books, Inc., 1973).

of political officials, so today we must do likewise. And one must admit that it is quite easy to slip into this simplistic mode of thought especially in these days when political corruption, rising taxes, and bureaucratic waste and theft of public moneys are in the news almost daily.

But we do not live under a monarchy in the seventh century B.C. Our system of government allows for voting out of office persons whom we think are bad for our government and whose interests are centered only in themselves. This was a privilege that the biblical writers had not experienced. It is, therefore, somewhat more difficult to know exactly how to apply the teachings of Jeremiah in our times. Having said that, however, it is surely true that the basic ideas and principles that Jeremiah held about the leaders of his own time can be applied to people in positions of leadership today. Honesty, integrity, a strong trust in God, and a genuine concern for the people and their well-being are just as relevant today as they were in 600 B.C. It is not that the principles cannot be applied; they definitely can. The question for us is how best to express our views and how best to act in such a way as to be able to be an instrument of change for the better. Jeremiah acted as one would in his time and place. We should learn how to act appropriately in our time and place.

An additional point can be examined in looking at Jeremiah's thinking about foreign nations. Again we are not able to formulate a one-to-one, across-the-board application of Jeremiah's teaching on this subject to our time. Jeremiah viewed the nations, however, as subject to Yahweh in much the same way as Judah was. Those nations could be and were used by Yahweh in his larger plans for his purpose for the world. And they were also subject to punishment for their sins and immoralities. But there was hope reflected even for the foreign nations; some of them would be restored after their punishment (i.e., Moab, Ammon, and Elam, and possibly Egypt).

While there is no specific guideline given for the standards by which the nations are judged or are restored or may be used in the plan of Yahweh for the world, and this is disappointing to some, it seems clear that, as far as Jeremiah was concerned, Yahweh is God over all the nations. And it is in accord with Yahweh's will that all the nations live together in peace, mutually supporting one another. The world being what it is, however, makes it possible for God to use certain nations to punish other nations, as with Babylonia and Judah. It would seem then that foreign nations have to be a concern of the truly religious person. Even in those days isolationism could not be a guiding principle for a nation in this world. Nations must relate to one another, and that relationship should be one of building up, not tearing down.

One final note and we shall be finished. Jeremiah found hope despite a wretched and lonely life for himself and a horrible fate which happened to his nation. This hope was rooted and grounded in the firm conviction which he had that God was a strength and power of such magnitude and had a personality which looked for positive goals. No amount of despair could dispel the confidence that Jeremiah had in God that ultimately God's people would be a significant and powerful force in the world. In spite of his own tragic life his words are still studied and are a source of inspiration to generation after generation.

Religious thinking in many areas has expanded greatly since Jeremiah's time. Some would say that God's revelation has gone far beyond some of the ideas that Jeremiah held. And in some ways this may be true. But if real religion is trust in God and commitment to God, no one anywhere can claim to be a more religious person than Jeremiah was. And in spite of all the tragedies of his own life, Jeremiah's integrity and faith still serve as an inspiration and a challenge for those of us who live almost 2,600 years later. He was truly a person who committed his life to the proposition that wherever matters of God were involved he was to be involved too!

Questions for Further Study

What are several places where the application of Jeremiah's teachings would be appropriate in our society today? In the church? In individual lives?

Bibliography

Achtemeier, Elizabeth, *Deuteronomy, Jeremiah.* Proclamation Commentaries. Philadelphia: Fortress Press, 1978.

Bright, John, ed., *Jeremiah.* Anchor Bible. Vol. 21. New York: Doubleday & Co., Inc., 1965.

Cunliffe-Jones, Hubert, *The Book of Jeremiah: Introduction and Commentary.* Torch Bible Commentaries. New York: Macmillan, Inc., 1961.

Holladay, William L., *Jeremiah: Spokesman Out of Time.* Philadelphia: United Church Press, 1974. Pilgrim Press Book.

Hyatt, James Philip, "The Book of Jeremiah: Introduction and Exegesis." *The Interpreter's Bible,* ed. G. A. Buttrick et al. Vol. 5. Nashville: Abingdon Press, 1956.

Leslie, Elmer A., *Jeremiah.* Nashville: Abingdon Press, 1954.

Nicholson, E. W., *The Book of the Prophet Jeremiah: Chapters 1-25.* The Cambridge Bible Commentary on the New English Bible. Cambridge: Cambridge University Press, 1973.

_____, *The Book of the Prophet Jeremiah: Chapters 26-52.* The Cambridge Bible Commentary on the New English Bible.

Cambridge: Cambridge University Press, 1975.

Raitt, Thomas M., *A Theology of Exile: Judgment/Deliverance in Jeremiah and Ezekiel.* Philadelphia: Fortress Press, 1977.

Three older works which are somewhat dated but are of real value in understanding Jeremiah's thought are:

Peake, A. S., *Jeremiah.* The Century Bible. 2 Vols. Edinburgh: T. & T. Clark, 1910-12.

Skinner, John, *Prophecy and Religion: Studies in the Life of Jeremiah.* New York: Cambridge University Press, 1922. Paperback edition, 1961.

Smith, G. A., *Jeremiah.* 4th Edition. New York: Harper & Row, Publishers, Inc., 1929.